by LOIS LORD

Bank Street College of Education, New York City.

collage and construction in school

PRESCHOOL / JUNIOR HIGH

LIBRARY OF CONGRESS Catalogue Number: 58-9168

SBN 87192-007-7

Printing History:

Copyright 1958
by DAVIS PUBLICATIONS, INC.
Worcester, MA, U.S.A.
Fifth and Revised Edition—1970

Reprinted by Bank Street College of Education—1996

table of contents

acknowledgments

All photographs, unless otherwise credited, are by **Soichi Sunami**
Design and typography by **Robert Wirth**

I want to thank all the teachers and institutions who have contributed children's work or photographs for this book. In gathering illustrative material I have tried to represent different kinds of schools. I have discussed with many teachers their particular schools so that suggestions in the book would be adaptable to a variety of teaching situations in large or small classes.

Many of the ideas expressed have been evolved as a result of working with elementary and junior high school students at The New Lincoln School, New York. I have been fortunate in teaching in this school where the art program is important because it has received increasing understanding and support from the administration and the teachers.

I am also most grateful for my association with the Children's Classes of the People's Art Center of the Museum of Modern Art, New York, where the creative approach to collage and construction as art forms for children has been pioneered.

I want also to thank all my friends and colleagues who have given me encouragement and help in many ways. I give thanks especially to the following educators for their valuable suggestions:

Victor D'Amico, Director, Department of Education, Museum of Modern Art, New York.
Jane Cooper Bland, Instructor, Children's Classes, Museum of Modern Art, New York.
Edgar S. Bley, Coordinator of the Middle School, The New Lincoln School, New York.
Dorothy Knowles, Instructor, Children's Classes, Museum of Modern Art, New York.
Edith L. Mitchell, formerly, State Director of Art Education, Delaware.
John H. Niemeyer, President, Bank Street College of Education, New York.

Lois Lord, *New York, May 1970*

Twenty-five years have passed since the original publication of this extraordinary book; yet it remains fresh and pertinent, a timely reminder in this age of computers that actual "experiential" reality holds untold wonders. Lois Lord takes us on a journey into classrooms, into the hearts, minds, and imaginations of children as they work with materials. In ways that are breathtakingly rich and illuminating she shows us, through encounters in collage and construction, how children learn to organize and express their ideas and deepest feelings about themselves and their worlds. Prompted by a natural inclination to explore, nurtured by insightful and sensitive teaching, Lois Lord demonstrates how children and young adolescents transform materials into personal visual languages in which they speak to us clearly and directly.

This language, we note, is not limited to the gifted and talented but emerges as the heritage of all children. As verbal language arises from natural inclination to exercise vocal cords accompanied by the joy in discovering ownership of sounds, so visual language emerges from tactile and kinesthetic experiences of surfaces, spaces, and movements in the child's world. Very young children make exploratory forays into everyday materials such as paper, wood, wire, and sand, and find deep satisfaction in composing spaces and surfaces that sit, stand, move, and express ideas. Visual ideas, as Lois Lord reveals to us, evolve from these elementary explorations of the world; collages and constructions are born from natural inclinations of the heart and mind to fashion meaning into forms, with thoughtful hands serving as tools for the aesthetic imagination.

Above all, Lois Lord speaks to teachers and parents. She reminds us that we are collaborators in awakening and sustaining into adolescence young peoples' encounters with materials. With a sensitive understanding of development to guide us, collecting materials can be a shared and joyful activity, and leading focused discussions of possibilities offers us the privilege of nurturing children's visual voices. Again and again throughout this book, Lois Lord insists that individual children must be encouraged to work in their own ways, to form and trust their own preferences and aesthetic judgment. She asks us not to divorce children from the larger world of art, and shows how we might help them form bridges to the works of artists such as Calder, Giacometti, Picasso, Schwitters, and many others. She offers caring advice to teachers on how to work with children who lack basic experiences in working with materials, on how to "catch them up." But most of all, she offers a wealth of specific suggestions for teachers to help them include collage and construction in their art curriculums and shows how thoughtful motivations can lead to rich experiences for young people, prekindergarten through junior high school.

This is a rare book, inspired by love of materials and deep insight about their role in shaping children's artistic-aesthetic voices into the adolescent years. More subtly, this book is written with a compelling generosity of spirit by a teacher-scholar who is able to breathe life and reality into the insights, examples, and supportive advice she offers. This book should touch a chord in the hearts of teachers and parents and should be on bookshelves across the nation, for it offers thoughtful examples of what art education can accomplish. The teaching of Lois Lord has had profound influence on those of us fortunate enough to come under her guiding and unfailingly generous hand. It seems right and natural that a new generation of teachers and artists should come under her spell; for the integrity of her insights and richness of her knowledge about the natural inclinations of children are needed even more urgently in this world today than they were twenty-five years ago.

Judith M. Burton
Teachers College, Columbia University
January 1995

children explore

with their senses

the world of

simple things.

Photos: Hella Hammid

when children go out to play

they often gather things they find.

they select some of these

and build them into new forms.

the selecting and building

is a spontaneous art experience.

Photo: Hella Hammid

children explore . . . select . . . create

Children explore with their senses the world of simple things. The delight of the child in his world is intense. It is an adventure for him to explore, then learn all he can about what is around him. He learns not only by looking but by feeling as well.

Children naturally select from things they find to make their own creations. This book is devoted to this aspect of the child's innate creativity, in which he selects, then puts together many things in two and three dimensions.

Children create in many ways. A child may draw shapes with a stick in the soft ground or with a piece of dry clay on the sidewalk. He may build a structure with sticks and other objects or he may put together bits of cardboard, paper or cloth to carry out an imaginative idea. Sometimes he works alone; at other times, like the children on the previous page, he works with companions. Watching the child closely we observe that he puts whole-hearted effort into these spontaneous creations, deriving from them deeply felt satisfaction. This book suggests some of the ways this kind of childhood experience can be transposed into the classroom and how the teacher can help children develop it for important learning.

Teachers have the opportunity to help children develop their natural gifts so they may become adults who are imaginative and warm human beings who respond to people, experiences and their environment spontaneously and with sensitivity. Because direct experience in creative art gives children the opportunity to foster and develop these qualities it should be an important part of the curriculum in every school.

The teacher's part is exciting because he has the opportunity to inspire children and give them guidance so they acquire gradually the disciplines necessary to all learning. To create with art materials, children must develop self-discipline that will enable them to make sensitive and independent choices and maintain a spontaneous approach as they develop in maturity, knowledge and technical skill.

It excites the imagination of every boy and girl to work in a wide variety of art materials. It is important that each child be given the opportunity to develop to his utmost, in his own direction.

Collage is a two-dimensional expression which nurtures a child's natural desire to touch, because he uses actual materials of varying texture and pattern to create his own designs. Working in collage can enrich the child's experience in painting in that it helps him to become aware of ways in which he can relate shapes, textures, patterns and colors on a flat surface.

Construction, because it is three-dimensional, will enlarge a child's concepts of form and space relationships. Construction offers a special opportunity for invention because a variety of materials can be put together in so many ways to create new forms.

Much has already been written about the way children work with paints and clay. This book offers teachers further possibilities for the creative growth of their pupils through collage and construction. When they are an integral part of the art program, collage and construction can offer boys and girls an exciting challenge and an opportunity for continually deepening experiences.

collage

Grade 1, Nichols School,
Macon County, Alabama.

Photo: Lois Lord

collage

A collage is a picture made by applying different materials to a flat surface. The word "collage" comes from the French word "coller," meaning to paste or stick. Even young children enjoy knowing this derivation.

As an art expression, collage was developed in France during the early part of this century by the artists Pablo Picasso and Georges Braque, and in Germany by Kurt Schwitters. In the United States, Arthur Dove made collages which expressed his feelings about such subjects as *Grandmother* and *Goin' Fishing.* Collage resulted, in part, from an effort to use, in art expression, the intrinsic beauty of every-day materials: bits of wood, discarded railway tickets, scraps of newspaper and cloth, and other objects. Collage was further developed in Germany at the Bauhaus, an experimental school of art whose teaching has stimulated many of our American artists and teachers.

Making collages is something that fundamentally belongs to children, too. It is not new for children to search out, collect and play with different materials but using them for an art form in school is comparatively new.

Some collages are abstract and emphasize contrasts of materials, like the one below, in others, materials are used to suggest a subject, as in Mary's *Lady,* right.

One way that children, from infancy on, explore their world is by touching. Collage encourages them to cultivate this way of finding out what materials are like. Developing the sense of touch in their fingers will enable boys

Collage by Robert, 8 years; Museum of
Modern Art Classes, New York.

and girls, when they use their eyes, to perceive more clearly the variety of surfaces they may encounter in everyday life. Collecting and using materials of different textures, colors and patterns may help them also to become the kind of adults who respond sensitively to their surroundings. They may learn to see more than just a building; to be aware that besides a structure they see complex relationships of rough, smooth and shiny surfaces. They may realize that a tree has a relationship of textures; the rough indented bark and the hard branches contrasting with the smooth or soft leaves. Through collage, children can be helped to see beauty in ordinary things and to grow in resourcefulness by appreciating the possibilities of using simple materials for art expression. Selecting materials for collage not only gives children intense pleasure, but also gives them an opportunity to make independent choices.

Because he uses different materials in making a collage, a child can learn to organize directly his visual and tactile responses, creating new forms and images. In collage, it is possible to change shapes and move them around until a satisfying arrangement has been achieved. This flexibility often helps the timid child who is afraid to start a painting or drawing; it can help all children develop awareness of design organization, a fundamental in art expression.

Materials sometimes inspire ideas. The idea for Mary's *Lady* came to her as she studied the materials which were available. The cardboard egg divider suggested the hat and the pebbly paper became the face. The blue metallic paper of the eyes was repeated in the shoes and contrasts with a rich variety of textures in the clothes. The result is a personal expression of great originality.

Collage materials may be combined in numerous ways. At times it is wise to offer many materials so that children learn how to choose from a variety to carry out a particular idea. At other times it is desirable to present only a few materials so that pupils have the opportunity to explore each one more fully.

Lady, by Mary, 8 years; New Lincoln School, New York. Mary pasted the materials to the background, then cut out the figure.

There is a developmental progression in the way children work in collage. Young children and beginners are usually interested primarily in exploring and feeling materials. They spontaneously select, arrange and paste material to a background. As they grow in age and experience, children become more thoughtful and their collages are more carefully planned. Experienced junior high school students often cut and arrange unusual shapes in subtle relationship to each other.

Collage is a medium which can be continuously used to provoke deeper learning throughout the school years, and afterwards. If it is approached in this way collage will not become a mere device or novelty.

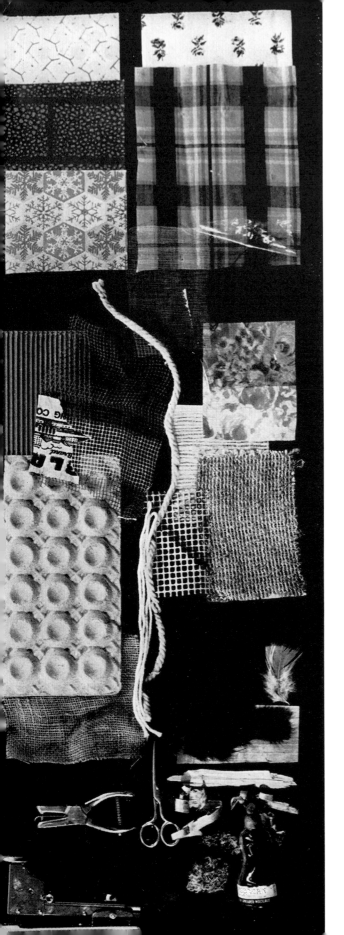

materials
for collage

A wide variety of materials should be kept on hand for collage. Some special ones may be bought but many scrap materials are both beautiful and useful. Collecting these materials awakens both teacher and pupils to textures and patterns around them and also extends a classroom activity into everyday life.

Class discussion can inspire children to seek out materials appropriate for collage. After pupils have talked about patterns and textures in the schoolroom and in the clothes they are wearing, a teacher might ask, "Where could you find some rough, smooth, shiny or patterned materials that you can bring to school to paste on paper or cardboard?" Answers might include: materials left from sewing, objects usually discarded, things found in the garden and the woods. In addition, storekeepers are often happy to save wrapping and packing materials for local schools. It is usually a good idea for children to have one experience with collage before they start searching for materials.

It is important always to have available contrasting, textured materials. Those which are rough include corrugated cardboard and burlap (bought or salvaged). Also to be found as scrap are used sandpaper, wood shavings, egg-crate dividers, excelsior, and orange, onion and potato sacks. Contrasting soft textures include pieces of fabric, velvet, scraps of fur, cotton, bits of sponge and feathers. Bright, small feathers are obtainable from millinery shops.

Smooth textures include shiny metallic papers, bought or salvaged from Christmas wrappings or from candy and other packets. Thin metals can be used by experienced children about eight years old.

Patterned materials are also important. In choosing them a word of caution must be given. Because the shapes children make should be of their own invention, pictorial designs should be avoided lest pupils be tempted simply to cut out houses, trees or animals made by others. Therefore, choose a variety of patterns in striped and other allover designs. Wallpaper sample books offer a wide selection of large and small motifs and often are given away at stores where wallpaper is sold. In addition, one can easily find wrapping papers and fabrics in a variety of patterns.

Transparent materials include colored cellophanes and sheets of colored gelatin. Nets, veilings and laces are transparent as well as having textures of their own. From theatrical fabric stores one can buy tarlatan and theatrical gauzes in vivid colors.

Some papers are translucent. One can buy colored tissue paper, preferably in brilliant colors, or collect the purple, orange and yellow tissue in which fruit is wrapped.

Small objects such as buttons, toothpicks and fluted bon-bon cups are useful in collage. Also, all sorts of ribbons, strings, yarn, rickrack, carpet wool and laces can be used to make lines and thin shapes.

Then, there is much that can be gathered from nature: dried leaves, moss, berries, seed pods, grasses, pine needles, small shells and sand, which can be sprinkled onto glue or paste.

For backgrounds, one needs paper, colored or white, or cardboard (shirt boards, box tops or cardboard from cartons are excellent).

Brushes or small sticks should be provided for pasting since it becomes too difficult to handle the materials if fingers are used for paste. Paintbrushes will not be harmed if washed out immediately after they are used in paste. Some people find it convenient to use mucilage with a rubber dispenser; rubber cement may also be used. The new milk-base glues are especially satisfactory for sticking wood shavings, bits of metal and small objects. It is good to have available paper fasteners and, for older students, pins and thumbtacks.

Long-armed staplers are desirable but not essential. Scissors should, if possible, be provided for each child.

It is essential to keep collage materials in good order so they are respected and readily available. They may be kept in shoe boxes labeled in such categories as rough, smooth, shiny, patterned, transparent, small objects, and strings. A box called "mixed bits" may also be included which can be a treasure trove for a few pupils to explore and select from when no special materials have been set out.

If storage space is limited, labeled shopping bags can be hung on hooks in the classroom or closet. In some art rooms materials are kept in labeled drawers; in others tote trays are used (procurable from school furniture houses). Oaktag folders are useful for large sheets of patterned and other papers.

Two second-graders work at collage near shelves which hold materials in labeled shoe boxes.

Photo: Hella Hammid

Grade 1, New Lincoln School, New York. Photo: Lois Lord

suggestions for teachers

In presenting collage it is important to set out materials, collected by the teacher and children, in an inviting way so each child will be inspired to make a thoughtful selection. The teacher will be guided in setting out the materials by the age of the children as well as by the physical conditions of the classroom.

Most three- and four-year-olds work rapidly pasting each piece of material as they choose it. Therefore materials should be within easy reach of each child. The photo (lower right) shows a three-year-old making a collage with a variety of textured materials. The teacher had provided each child with a box top containing a variety of small pieces from which to choose.

By the time children are five or six they generally pre-plan their work to the extent that they can choose an assortment of materials then arrange and paste them. Therefore in elementary and junior high school materials may be arranged away from the working space. Boys and girls choose, then take what they have selected back to their places. Mate-

rials may be set out in trays (as in photo, upper right) or box tops. In a classroom with small desks, materials could be arranged for selection on those in the front row and then cleared away when the children are ready to work, or, if necessary, the trays could be laid in a row on the floor. Materials may be grouped according to their texture or pattern quality. For example, on one tray rough materials, on another smooth, and another bumpy, another soft, etc.

Merely to set out materials is not enough. The teacher decides what materials to put out for the day's lesson. Too great a variety is confusing, yet there must be enough so that each boy and girl may make his own selection. If a child wants something that is not included he may get it from the collage storage. The teacher does not give exact directions but must encourage every boy and girl to explore the materials by touch and sight so that they can make the most sensitive selections possible. A brief discussion before class will help children to focus and choose those

16

materials they would like to use together.

The picture on page 16 shows a teacher and first-grade children looking at and discussing materials for collage. Even though these children had worked with collage before they enjoyed closing their eyes and feeling the materials. "This one feels rough and scratchy," said Billy as he felt some rough bark. Then the teacher held up the piece of bark so that after feeling it the children could study its appearance and see how the texture made a pattern on it. They discussed the many gradations of texture from soft to rough and how a variety of materials felt to the touch and appeared to the eyes.

The children were soon ready to choose materials. The illustration at the top of this page shows two children discussing a material as they make their selections from the trays with various textures the teacher has set out on a table. After they had chosen their materials, each child decided upon a background, either grey or brown cardboard or colored construction paper.

When the children start to work the teacher gives guidance to those who need it. Some children may need technical advice as, for example, a child may need a suggestion to use more paste to make a heavy material stick, while another may need the suggestion to wipe off the paste brush so as not to use too much. Some children may need encouragement in making their own arrangements. A child may ask, "What shall I put here?" To him the teacher might say, "Do you want to repeat a material you already have in your picture, or introduce something new? Which would look better to you?" Children should always feel free to go back to the choosing table to get more materials if they need them.

This general approach to the teaching of the art of collage, in which the teacher sets the stage and guides the pupils toward seeing and using materials in a vital, individual way, will work equally well with all elementary and junior high school classes.

Photo: Lois Lord

Grade 1, New Lincoln School, New York.

Zachery, 3 years, New Lincoln School, New York.
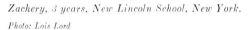
Photo: Lois Lord

Collages (6" x 9") by Dexter and Steven, 3 years, Bank Street School for Children, New York. Dexter (above) chose only two pieces of fabric while Steven (below) pasted textured pieces in many layers.

William, 4 years, Bank Street School, New York.

collage in preschool
and kindergarten

Photos in this section by Lois Lord

The very young child explores and learns a great deal through his sense of touch. Making collages therefore seems natural because it evolves from his elementary exploration of his world.

Collage is important among the art experiences which provide the young child with opportunities for many learnings necessary by the time he reaches grade one. He learns how to put things in categories, as well as new vocabulary, while he decides which materials are rough, smooth, soft, etc. He learns to make his own choices as he selects what he will use for his collage. He develops skills as he learns to cut or paste. Making collages helps a child to concentrate on creating his own order as he arranges what he has selected. The very young child works so fast that it is hard to see that he is arranging, yet as the products of different children are compared it becomes evident that they have been arranged in a wide variety of ways.

Cutting and pasting are two separate activities for three- and some four-year-olds and should be offered at different times or at separate tables. Cutting is a challenging skill for threes to master and an activity that they enjoy tremendously.

In both preschool and kindergarten a teacher can expose children to a series of consecutive collage experiences in which the combination of materials and the sequence in which they are presented stimulate learning through discovery. After the children have made paper collages, textured papers can be added, then

corrugated, patterned papers, etc. When young children become familiar with the materials they will notice when something new is added. The teacher can reinforce each discovery by her attention. As fabrics and other textures are introduced attention will be focused on touching. Colored cellophanes used either alone or with colored papers stimulate learning of color and color mixing. There is no formula for a good sequence of collage experiences but each teacher must develop one for her group as she is guided by the response of the children and by the work they do. Paper only should be provided for the cutting experience, since few young children can cut cloth. It is completely satisfying for them to cut colored paper into little pieces and then pile them up. Pasting takes longer to master than cutting. Brushes must be provided with the paste so that fingers remain clean to enable the child to enjoy textures and so that he can have more control in arranging his collage. Few preschool children are ready to combine pasting and cutting. When they are ready they will do so if paste and scissors are available.

Because three- four- and five-year-olds make such rapid choices and do not pre-plan their work, a tray or box top with a selection of materials should be within the reach of every child as he works (as in the illustration left). The materials should be pre-cut in very simple small shapes in a variety of proportions (as in the collages on these pages). Shapes should not be geometric or contrived "free-form" shapes which suggest adult work. For backgrounds small paper about 9″ x 12″ or 6″ x 9″ should be provided.

In introducing collage it is wise to give three-year-olds many opportunities to work only with pre-cut colored papers because they

Animal (10″ long) by Charlotte, 5 years, Early Childhood Center of Bank Street College, New York. Charlotte stapled pieces of pre-cut cardboard together to make this animal then added collage materials. Later she attached a stick to make it into a puppet.

Collage (6″ x 9″) by Chris, 5 years, Divens School, Elmira, New York. Chris chose two pieces of a patterned material which he arranged in relation to small pieces of smooth and shiny materials.

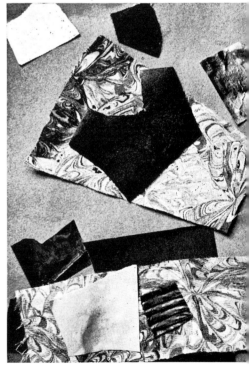

Person (14″ wide) by Peter, 5 years, New Lincoln School, New York. Peter assembled the materials three-dimensionally to make this original symbol of a person. Eyes, nose and mouth are almost concealed by the goggles made from a strip of egg carton.

Torn paper collage (12″ x 18″) by Roderick, 5 years,
Bradley School, Huntsville, Alabama.
Roderick used colored paper to express part of a story
which was read in his kindergarten.

are mostly involved in learning to paste. Three-year-olds generally brush the paste on the paper background smearing it around with pleasure before putting the pre-cut pieces on it. Often they will put more paste on top of the pieces they have arranged and add another layer. If a child seems to need help, the teacher can show him how to press a piece of paper to the paste on the background. After the children have had some experience the teacher may show the way to put paste on the back of each piece to be pasted but children should not be forced to do it this way before they understand and want to, which may not be until they have had considerable experience or are older.

The collages on page 18 demonstrate two ways three-year-olds are apt to work. Both boys worked rapidly, Dexter successively making several collages using only a few pieces on each while Steven kept adding layers to his as though making a series of superimposed collages. Each boy was learning in his own way how to organize.

Three-year-olds gain confidence by repeating experiences, therefore they should have the opportunity to work many times with the same materials before more textures or patterns are gradually added. By four, children can concentrate longer and are more selective. However, four- or even five-year-olds with no previous experience may work like threes. Many experiences with collage may help them to become thoughtful and aware in learning to organize shapes.

Kindergarten children with experience will rapidly acquire skill in pasting and cutting and some notion of pre-planning. Their longer attention span will make possible some discussion. For example, before making texture collages, the teacher may plan a short discussion. While the children have their eyes closed, she might pass around bits of material of contrasting textures for them to feel. "Do these feel the same or different?" "Is it rough, smooth, scratchy or soft?" she asks. This will encourage them to respond to the quality of surface rather than merely naming the object. Then she might say, "Each of you choose the textures you would like to use together in your design."

Toward the end of the kindergarten year, children may be ready to select their collage materials from a choosing table and then take

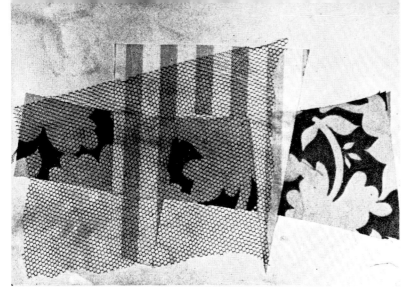

Collage (6″ x 9″) by Rose-Marie, 5 years,
Union Settlement, New York.
From many materials Rose-Marie selected two pieces
of patterned fabric. Then she cut the piece
of net to go over them, organizing her
design in an interesting way.

Elephant at the Zoo (6″ x 9″) by Lucas, 5 years,
New Lincoln School, New York.
The coarse net on his collage suggested
a cage to Lucas so he put
the elephant inside.

them to the working space as suggested on page 16.

During kindergarten most children learn to draw and paint symbols. Sometimes collage materials inspire originality in symbol making, like *Man* (on page 19) which Peter made spontaneously. A teacher could give an open-ended motivation like, "Would you like to use these materials to make a person or an animal?" Charlotte's animal (page 19) was made following a motivation by a teacher who felt that her five- and six-year-olds needed some stimulation to go ahead in symbol-making. She put out collage materials and piles of cardboard, pre-cut in small rectangles of varying sizes and proportions. She said, "Could you find a way to put these card-boards together to make a person or an animal?" The majority of children quickly used the pieces, creating symbols of people or animals, spontaneously applying collage materials to both sides. Later, sticks were attached so that they became puppets. The few children who were not ready for this project made collage designs. Every child in preschool and kindergarten should be encouraged to work in his own way.

Collages (6" x 9") by Hosa and Gloria, grade 1,
Prairie Farms School, Macon County, Alabama.
Hosa made a bold design using
a few pieces of contrasting fabric
while Gloria, working at the same time,
grouped with care the small pieces
she cut, making a subtle arrangement.

collage in grades one and two

Because collage gives children the opportunity to develop the sense of touch as well as enjoyment of pattern and color, the tactile approach is a good beginning whether or not they have had previous experience. As suggested for kindergarten, a suitable motivation is one in which children feel various materials with their eyes closed. The teacher encouraged them to discuss contrasts and similarities in texture. The teacher might then make the transition to working by saying, "Which of these textures would each of you like to arrange next to each other in your design?"

Each child must be encouraged to work in his own way. Some choose many materials while others choose only a few. Some like to arrange large pieces while others prefer small ones. The two collages above were made at the same time. Hosa made an interesting arrangement of apparently three pieces (he has covered a dark bit on the right with a light one and the texture shows through). Gloria, on the other hand, cut up the soft felt, fur and sponge she has chosen, arranging the bits in groups.

Children should gradually develop the ability to select and arrange materials more thoughtfully. One way the teacher can give them subtle guidance is by offering at successive lessons a wider variety of materials. Children, at first, should not be confused by having too many things from which to choose, yet there should be enough variety to enable each one to choose a different combination.

When patterned surfaces are introduced, children discover the difference between materials that feel similar but look different. Pat-

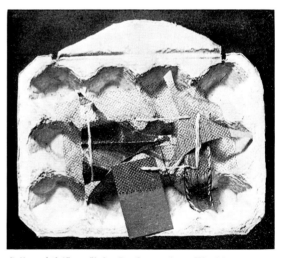

Collage (5½" x 6") by Paula, grade 1; Washington
School, Oakland, California. Three bits of shiny paper,
a piece of net and one of ribbon are attached with
string, instead of paste, to a rough-textured egg box.

*Collage (12" x 20") by Jane, grade 1,
New Lincoln School, New York.
Jane first chose two pieces of bark
and then the soft fur, velvet,
and sponge in contrast. She made
her design a dramatic contrast of
light and dark, pattern and texture.*

*Self Portrait (8" x 13") by Kay, grade 2; Parkvale
School, Hastings, New Zealand. Kay made this self
portrait from different kinds of cloth which she
stitched to a plain cloth background. She added
details with needle and thread.*

terned fabrics or papers may be offered in combination with plain-colored paper or cloth, or metallic papers or with textured or transparent materials.

Some children continue through elementary school to prefer to make collages which are designs without subject matter, while quite early others will choose materials to express ideas. With motivation centered on the nature of materials and how they can be related in a picture, each child should feel free to do that which is natural for him. The teacher can guide him to grow in understanding by comments on his choices and arrangements. For example, he might say, "It is very nice the way you have arranged these materials in groups and made big shapes by having little shapes touching each other."

A motivation "Big and Little" will help children to focus in ways of arranging large and small shapes on a flat surface. Some chil-

Bakery (12" x 18") by Caitlin, Grade 1, New Lincoln School, New York. After a class trip Caitlin expressed her impression of the bakery. She grouped small bits of soft and shiny material on top of the two large areas of pattern and rough texture.

dren will make designs, others will work out the problem in terms of a subject—mother and child, animal with baby animals, or an animal or person with large objects like buildings or trees.

Scissors should always be available, though at first young children may prefer to choose and paste pieces already cut. These should be very simple shapes. Children can best learn the technique of cutting when they work with a variety of colored and patterned papers. By second grade most children are able to cut their own shapes from many materials. With experience, children not only develop skill in the ability to use scissors but also in cutting subtle and individual shapes to use in their designs.

Collage (9" x 12") by Nancy, grade 2; Center School, New Canaan, Connecticut. Metallic paper, cotton and excelsior are combined with crayon to make this spirited collage of a horse running into a barn. Nancy has arranged the barn door so it will open.

Collage (12″ x 18″)
by Michelle, 8 years,
Early Childhood
Center, Bank
Street College,
New York.
Michelle chose
one patterned
fabric which
she cut and
arranged in
a thoughtful way
on overlapping
smooth and
soft materials.

collage in grades three and four

If third- and fourth-graders have not had previous collage experience they might start with textures, as suggested for younger children. If they have had experience, arranging materials with more conscious understanding can deepen their perception.

King (8″ x 11″) by Bob, grade 3; Irvington, New Jersey, Public Schools. "I wanted this to be a proud king," said Bob, who chose purple and red paper for robe and background, soft cotton for the hair and fur trimming, cork for the face and feet, and gold paper for the crown.

The teacher might encourage them to be selective by saying, "Which materials will you choose to use together? Do you want to use a few or many materials?" and, "It is a good idea to take several pieces of each material you choose because you may find you want to repeat a material in different parts of your picture."

Motivations should be broad enough to include those who use materials to make non-representational designs and also those who might want to suggest a subject. A teacher might say, "Here are some rough materials and some that are soft. What do the rough ones suggest to you? What do the soft, fluffy ones suggest?" Thus encouraged, the children may discuss ideas and think of different ways of using the materials. Bob made his *King*, lower left, after such a discussion.

At times the teacher may suggest that each pupil choose a subject and select materials he finds most suited to it. He could either make a design that expressed the feeling of the subject or a collage picture of it. To help the children the teacher might say, "Which of these materials reminds you of the feeling of a circus, a hot beach, a cool dark forest or a holiday?" Suggestions should be varied so that during the

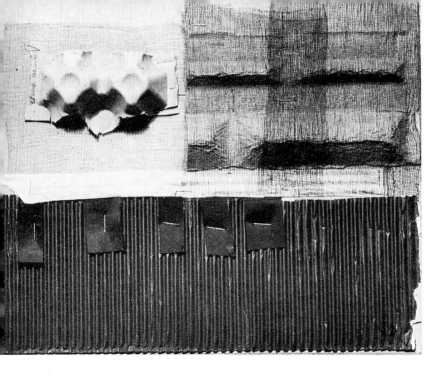

Collage (9½" x 12") by Barry,
9 years; Museum of Modern Art
Classes, New York. Barry called
his collage "Primitive Peoples in
Mountain Caves." He used egg-
box dividers for mountains and net
to suggest mist. He chose blue
corrugated cardboard for water and
stapled to it rectangles of paper
for wharves.

Cave Man (12" x 18") by Tommy, grade 3; New
Lincoln School, New York. Tommy used rough
wool for this cave man's clothing and for the load
he carries on his head. He combined paint with
the textured paper stapled to the background
to suggest the huts and landscape.

Collage (8½" x 12") by Tom W. and Tom S.
grade 3; Medill Elementary School, Newark,
Delaware. These two boys, who had not worked
together before, talked about the materials as
they chose them. As they started to cut
colored paper, textured cloth and tape, the
idea of "Shipwreck" developed and together
they arranged the materials, curling white
paper for the turbulent water.

Collage (9″ x 12″) by Robert, grade 4; Union Free School District No. 1, East Hampton, New York. Robert was very inventive in the way he cut and arranged shapes of one material. By combining and overlapping pieces of colored paper he created new shapes which give variety and unity to his design.

discussion each child will find something that is personal to him.

After a discussion about the contrasts between bumpy, smooth and patterned materials, Barry looked at a variety of them. Shapes of the egg crate dividers suggested mountains, so he developed the idea for the collage illustrated, top of Page 26; Tommy represented a similar subject, lower left, in his way which happened to be more realistic. To many others in both of these groups the materials suggested nonrepresentational designs.

Making people with collage materials helps children to gain confidence and develop ability in all media to make representations of the human figure. Parts of the body may be cut separately and moved until the desired action

is attained. Motivations such as "Running," "Hurrying," "Reaching," "Waving," may help each child develop his own subject with figures in action. Both boys and girls enjoy selecting and applying materials for clothing, accessories and background.

If possible, a group might be taken on a "searching" trip. This will awaken new possibilities in the use of materials as well as giving the children an opportunity to become more aware of their surroundings. In the country or woods they look for leaves, moss, bark and other things from nature that can later be used for collage. In the city, a trip to a grocery store could reveal many bright colored papers, corrugated cardboard, cellophane, excelsior and other packing materials.

Collage (6½″ x 8½″) by Karen, grade 4; Parkman School, Detroit, Michigan. Such a planned arrangement of materials is unusual for a child so young. Karen organized, with sensitivity and care, groups of different seeds, macaroni and raisins dropped on glue. For contrast she introduced shapes of textured and patterned materials.

Photo: Lois Lord

Collage (16" x 26") by John, grade 5; Central School, Pawling, New York. John collected feathers, burrs and bark and thoughtfully arranged them with many other textures in a box top to make a "Feeling box."

collage in grades five and six

The use of collage in fifth and sixth grades will depend on the previous experience of the children. If they are inexperienced, several lessons should be devoted to exploring and arranging textures and patterns as described earlier. Children who have had experience should be made to feel they are developing endless possibilities in the use of collage, not simply repeating previous experiences.

Children of ten often work with more knowledge of what they want to achieve than do younger children. Therefore, the teacher might encourage them to think more about contrasting qualities in materials and ways of selecting and arranging them. It is usually a good idea, with children over ten, not to hand out paste at the beginning of a class. This will encourage each child to move shapes around till he arrives at an arrangement that satisfies him.

Some children, naturally, make collages from many small pieces of material. Jean, whose collage is illustrated, top of facing page, intuitively grouped her figures made of small bits to form a unified design. By commenting on this arrangement, the teacher encourages further growth in Jean's own way of working. On the other hand some children work with many tiny shapes, not because it is their preference to do so, but because they lack courage in using materials. A teacher might help such a child by appreciating his selection and then asking, "Would you like to arrange some larger shapes along with your small ones, or group some small shapes to make a large one, or do you like your design the way it is?" If the child is satisfied, of course the teacher will accept his effort and then encourage him to experiment further. If he is not satisfied the

Street Scene (18″ x 24″) by Jean, grade 5; New Lincoln School, New York. In this lively collage, Jean has used a variety of textured and patterned cloth. She shows her experience in the way the figures are placed in space and by overlapping. She achieved quality of design in the way she placed the three large buildings and grouped the small figures around them.

teacher might also ask, "Would you like to use some long bits of string in your design, or would you prefer large shapes of cellophane or net under or over your small shapes?" The latter would point out possibilities in the use of transparencies as well as in overlapping. The teacher, by offering several possibilities, will leave the final decision to the child.

Other children, like Bob whose collage is below, work naturally with larger pieces. To them the teacher might also point out possibilities of grouping, overlapping and adding variety with line or small shapes.

In fifth and sixth grades some children will consistently do collages with subject matter, others prefer nonrepresentational designs, still

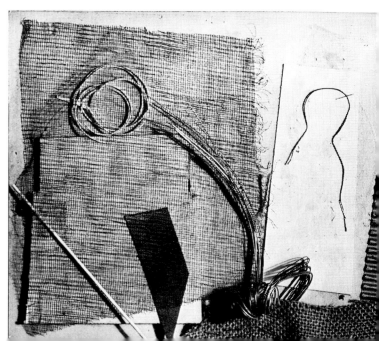

Collage (8″ x 10″) by Bob, grade 6; New Lincoln School, New York. Bob used contrasting textures for this subtle design. The small pieces of corrugated cardboard and burlap on the right balance the large piece of net placed over cardboard shapes at the left. The small curved piece of wire, stapled to cardboard on the right, echoes the bunch of wires twisted through the burlap and put over the net to the left.

Collage (18" x 24") by Robert, grade 6; Midtown Ethical Culture School, New York.
Robert made this design with cellophane and cut-up raffia, then he
enhanced it by adding line and texture with paint and chalk.

others will alternate between the two. It is important to set out interesting combinations of materials with plenty of large pieces (at least 9 by 12 inches) as well as small ones.

The subjects suggested for third and fourth grades would also be appropriate at this age level. One teacher of ten-year-olds started a discussion by saying, "Which of these materials suggests something gay?" The children searched out various combinations of materials, discussed them and the subjects they suggested. The teacher then added, "Which materials suggest something sad?" This brought further suggestions from the children and thus helped each to bring out his own idea.

Another teacher started by asking, "What kind of person does this rough sandpaper suggest to you? Does this soft velvet or this lace suggest a very different kind of person?" As a result of the discussion the following subjects were among those used: *Indians Beating Drums, Stylish Ladies, A Beggar in an Ugly Hut, Looking at his Dream House in the Country, Football Player, A Girl Standing in a Deep Forest.* Some children did designs, among them one called *Happiness,* composed of shiny papers, feathers and soft cloth.

A teacher can use the current interests of the students as motivation for their art. Collage materials can be used effectively by boys and girls to express their feelings about such subjects as: "Sports," "Dancing," "Rock Music Groups," "City of the Future," "Space Travel." Discussion should help each child to select materials and then arrange them to express his own particular feeling about the subject.

Photo: Lois Lord

Ninth graders work at collage;
New Lincoln School, New York.

collage in junior high school

Boys and girls who have had stimulating art experiences in elementary school can continue to use collage materials in a progressively thoughtful and discriminating way, through junior high school and beyond. Those with little previous art experience often approach collage with a freedom they lack in drawing and painting, in which media many children feel they cannot meet adult standards so frequently take refuge in clichés or copying.

By junior high school most boys and girls like to feel they are learning something about art as well as "doing." It is often hard for them to grasp the idea that there is no absolute right and wrong in art, but rather, that there are principles of design and the interpretation of these principles differs with each individual.

Collage is a useful means of exploring art principles. A study of two-dimensional design is easier in collage than in painting because the student works with actual shapes of material and can move them around until he achieves an arrangement that seems right to him.

For students to whom the medium is new the introduction to collage suggested for fifth- and sixth-graders would be suitable, although junior high school beginners may need more discussion and explanation to get started because they will want to know the values of what they do. They may want to know reasons for using collage and be given assurance that it is a recognized art medium. This age level has more sense of planning ahead.

Working out a design within limits may stimulate students experienced in collage. They might choose three or five materials from many, or work with one kind of shape such as curved or straight-edged, or spend more time arranging before finally pasting.

Design cannot be taught as a subject apart. Some students can best approach it through subject matter, others by working on abstract designs. Some subjects dictate particular kinds

Gay City (12″ x 18″) by Susan M., grade 7; New Lincoln School, New York.
Previous experience in collage enabled Susan thoughtfully to select
textures and colors and combine them in this subtle, sophisticated design
to express a gay city. She has not made a picture of a city but has
expressed its essence and a particular mood by overlapping rectangles
of contrasting textures and transparent nets. The irregular placement
of the shapes and the small bits of silver foil give a feeling of gaiety.

of shapes. For instance, in giving a problem involving rectangles, "A City" or "An Interior" might be suggested. "Hilly Country" or "A Forest" could inspire the use of curved shapes alone, or with straight shapes. Such subjects inevitably suggest overlapping one shape on another as shown in Susan's *City*, facing page, and Donald's *Jungle*, right.

Junior high school students are often intrigued by a word or phrase which allows for many different interpretations or can be expressed nonrepresentationally in a design. Some examples that have been used successfully are: escape, flight, party, confined, big and little and carnival. Alone and together suggests a subject or a design in which a single shape balances a group.

Many students enjoy and learn from making two collages expressing opposite feelings: "Happiness and Sadness," "Gaiety and Seriousness," "Work and Play," or "Noisy and Quiet." The teacher can point out the importance of choosing materials, shapes and arrangements that suggest the feeling to each student. The choice of colors and materials to express an emotion is really a personal matter. After collages are finished, students might enjoy discussing their choices.

In making collage portraits each student should be encouraged to choose the combination of materials which, to him, suggests the kind of person he wishes to portray. It might also be emphasized that collage is suitable for impression or exaggeration and not for realistic portraits. John's *King* (page 34) has a feeling of richness, owing to the juxtaposition of the materials used. Theresa's *Woman* has originality in the abstract way she placed the materials that form the shape of the face.

By ninth grade most students are ready to think seriously and consciously about qualities

Jungle (12″ x 18″) by Donald, grade 7; Friends' School, Germantown, Pennsylvania. This is Donald's first collage and the materials suggested a jungle to him. He intuitively created a well composed design by arranging the richly patterned treetops in contrast with the velvet, tweed and silk trunks and the plain areas of green background. The overlapping shapes help integrate his design.

of design. While successful visual organization involves many factors that cannot be isolated, teaching can help students to focus attention with increasing awareness on visual fundamentals. An organization of shapes, colors and textures which "works" is a highly individual matter. Working with different collage materials may lead students to discover

Portraits (12″ x 18″) grade 8; New Lincoln School, New York. These collage portraits show two individual ways of working. John's *King, left,* has a rich feeling owing to the contrast of the velvet beard and patterned crown, to the burlap face. The materials for the features are carefully chosen and simply placed. Theresa has arranged materials in a subtle and imaginative way to form her *Woman, right.* She used textured materials to divide the face in areas of light and dark.

the difference in attraction to the eye between dull and bright color or between plain and patterned materials.

A ninth grade was given a series of problems aimed to heighten the students' awareness of the organization of the picture surface through dealing in a variety of ways with the arrangement of positive and negative shapes. To explain the concept of positive and negative areas, the teacher placed a few pieces of white paper on a colored background. The white shapes represented the positive, and the re-

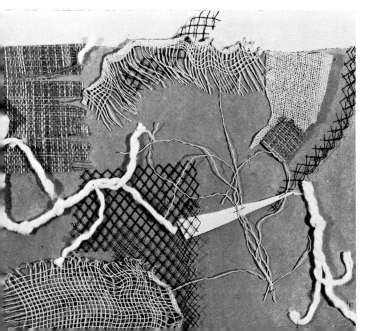

Happiness (12″ x 18″) by Susie, grade 9; New Lincoln School, New York. Susie made this sensitive arrangement after much trial and thought. She was inventive in using the threads she frayed from the net and in unwinding the heavy white yarn in order to make from it a rhythmic, linear design.

maining color around them the negative. The class found that in studying a drawing of a head, the head itself was the positive shape while the remaining background was the negative. When the drawing was held upside down students could disregard the subject while studying the shapes. Paintings which emphasize positive-negative design, such as Vermeer's *View of Delft* can be studied in similar manner so that students learn that some abstract principles apply equally to realistic painting.

In the first problem in a series, students were asked to make an abstract two-color torn-paper collage in which both positive and negative areas were equally interesting. To help the students to realize the importance of the negative, they were asked to tear and paste onto a piece of paper shapes which they thought of as negative. Raymond, in his collage (above), tore the light paper for negative areas, which made a design as interesting as the design of the positive areas. The result gives a particular tension on the picture surface. In this problem no limitation was placed on the kind of shapes. Some students chose to work with a few large shapes, while others worked with groups of smaller shapes. The various kinds of organization created by different students made the basis for a class discussion from which emerged discovery of ways in which feeling can be expressed by shapes and the way they are placed on the page. The discussion suggested succeeding problems which were carried out in three colors (Steve's collage, center right). Discussion also suggested that to achieve contrast in a design one must consider size, shape, color, value and interval. Some of the work was abstract and some suggested a subject (Jane's *Hands*, below right). Texture and pattern were introduced and finally the human figure. Even the least

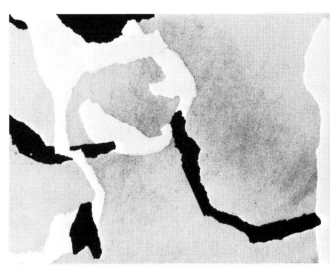

Paper Collages (18″ x 24″) by ninth graders, New Lincoln School, New York. Three sequential problems in organizing positive and negative shapes. Raymond (above) used two colors, while Steve (center) used three colors. Jane (lower) suggested a subject "Hands." In all three designs there is a strong tension between positive and negative areas.

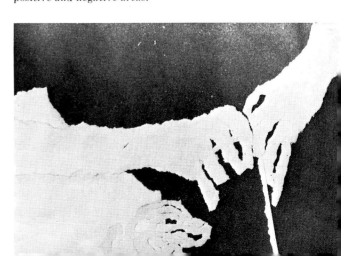

Photos: Lois Lord

Collage figures (20" high) by Stefanie (left) and Stanford (right), grade 9; New Lincoln School, New York. Both students interpreted the gesture of the posed figure in an individual way. Stefanie used textured and pat- terned materials to suggest clothing while Stanford used materials to emphasize the abstract quality of his design.

confident students were challenged when asked to sketch with chalk, paint or define with torn paper the negative areas around the figure, rather than actually attempting to draw one of their classmates. With emphasis on negative shapes they all developed more confidence as well as more accurate observation. In the final problem (illustrated above), students sketched in with paint the negative areas around the figure posed to emphasize gesture. Finally, the positive areas were re- emphasized by application of collage materials, a rich variety of textures and patterns having been provided. The two examples (above), the work of two students who differed in skill and approach, show that in this medium each was able to produce a strong and individual work.

Students are often helped to achieve more interesting and individual work in painting and other fields of art as a result of specifically thinking through a collage problem in design. Involvement in design problems may lead naturally to the study of great works of art. Many students will like to know that collage is a medium used by well-known artists, and that one can gain a richer understanding of the medium by studying collages by Braque, Picasso, Schwitters, Dove, Anne Ryan, Marca-Relli, and others.

Woman Knitting (18″ x 24″) by Betty, 14 years;
Museum of Modern Art Classes, New York. Within
an irregular pyramid Betty arranged triangles
of textured materials to suggest a woman, using thin and
thick wires to delineate the figure. The subtle rhythm
is the result of repetition with variation of shapes and lines.

construction:

Second-graders making constructions; New Lincoln
School, New York. Both Janet and Philip are deeply
involved in their creative work. Janet is making a small
delicate construction while Philip is working on a large
one. He has chosen wire, sticks, bits of cellophane and
strips of corrugated cardboard and has skillfully
attached them to make his well composed design.

Photo: Hella Hammid

stabiles and mobiles

A construction is a three-dimensional design made with one or many materials. It can be representational or abstract. The relationship between lines, shapes of solid or transparent material, and the shapes of the spaces between these materials makes up the design.

Constructions differ from traditional sculpture, which is carved or modeled out of a bulky material, in that the open areas are as important to the design as the solid shapes.

Many contemporary sculptors make constructions and they sometimes use such techniques as welding—new to sculpture. Their compositions are often built with metals such as steel or sometimes plastics are used, thus introducing transparency which creates an element of fluid space.

Sculptors who use this approach include Alberto Giacometti, Naum Gabo, Ibram Lassaw, David Smith and Isamu Noguchi. Artists of the Bauhaus also contributed to the concept of construction as art and a learning process.

Children of all ages have a natural aptitude for creating with three-dimensional media, perhaps more than we realize. Young children build with sand at the beach or with sticks in the woods. What they make often has the quality of art expression.

Constructions which remain fixed are called stabiles; those which are made to move are called mobiles.

Motion is fascinating to people of all ages. Children, especially, love to watch birds flying, leaves rustling in the wind or a piece of paper blowing down the street.

Motion itself has aesthetic appeal and it may have been this that led the contemporary artist Alexander Calder to make mobiles. His are complex and in them all parts move in various directions, setting up rhythms of motion and reverse motion.

Mobile by Jack, grade 8; Dover Special School District, Delaware. The free-moving parts on this delicately balanced mobile are made from plexiglass.

Young children, of course, are not able to make complex moving structures but creating something hanging in the air can be for them an adventure in invention and a source of delight. We can call these simple beginnings "hanging constructions."

Making many kinds of constructions and working with a variety of materials open different avenues for experimentation.

There are numerous three-dimensional materials, each with its own possibilities and limitations. Clay is one of these and is excellent for children of all ages but, if we believe that children should have three-dimensional experiences, we should expose them to many additional materials which have other kinds of possibilities and limitations. These experiences will add to their knowledge of materials and enable each boy and girl to find the kind of medium best suited to his expression.

Construction (12″ high) by Ned, 4 years, Bank Street School, New York.

The construction (right) was made by Bob who was familiar with clay and often made figures with it. On the day he made this piece he wanted to express an idea which demanded shapes he could not carry out completely in clay. He looked for other materials and chose wire to build up the curved shapes, and sticks to make the angular contrast and support the balls of clay which he stuck on them. Bob was familiar with many materials so he intuitively chose the sticks and wires from a sound structural motive. He created a design in which the materials and open spaces are related with sensitivity.

At times children modify their ideas to the dictates of the materials; at other times they choose materials to carry out ideas. Both of these disciplines are important.

Construction gives further opportunity to select and develop confidence in one's own ability to make choices. In collage, materials are selected to be organized on a flat surface. Choosing materials for a construction is a more complex problem. In deciding between a variety of materials and colors the student must consider not only the visual appeal (how they will look together) but also the structural problem of how they can be attached so they will hold together in a three-dimensional design. Since there are no prescribed ways of using the materials, making constructions offers a unique opportunity for inventiveness.

Philip, who is shown on Page 38 working on his construction, was involved in all these problems. As he was working he said, "Do you know what I do? I look and look at all these things till I see what I really want, then I choose it to put on my design." He then curved a long strip of yellow corrugated cardboard and attached it to the wires.

Making constructions gives children the opportunity to become aware of space-form relationships. A young child explores and experiences space with his body when he climbs a tree or a jungle-gym. This is kinaesthetic learning: the perception of bodily movement in space. However, understanding space and knowing whether there is room to get between the branches of a tree and knowing that the spaces between the branches have volume can be more than practical knowledge; it becomes an aesthetic experience when the whole relationship between volumes of groups of leaves and volumes of space between them is perceived as one design. By creating a variety of three-dimensional forms themselves, children can become sensitive to this kind of space relationship.

Up to about the age of eight children usually have an intuitive understanding of space-form relationships. Unless this understanding is cultivated it appears to diminish as they grow older. Few adults are aware that these relationships exist in architecture or everyday objects.

Young people can put to work and develop a feeling for structure when creating in three-dimensional media. Most children have built with blocks. This is building with weight and balance without permanent joints. Making wood constructions in which pre-cut pieces are glued or nailed offers another experience. Ned, four years, was deeply involved as he chose and arranged shapes for his construction above. Other kinds of structural problems can be added; for example, how a slender material like wire can support weight and how paper or metal can be bent to support itself or other materials.

The opportunity for invention in solving structural problems is extended by making hanging constructions. Paul's hanging construction shown on Page 51 is well constructed for the purpose of hanging, yet it would collapse were it placed on a table. Through working in the air children become more aware of the principle of balance. Often, by about the age of ten, children increase the complexity of their constructions by suspending small parts which move within the whole.

Working with a variety of three-dimensional materials develops special skill in using one's hands as the tool of the imagination. The skill and imagination demonstrated by some young children have amazed many adults when they themselves try to use similar materials. When, in order to interpret the art program to parents, a workshop was held in an elementary school, one father, as he worked on a construction, remarked, "This is hard to do. I had no idea what went into the art work that Bruce and Mary bring home."

In some constructions the emphasis is on the relationship of solid shapes and the space shapes between them. In others, the emphasis is on line and the open space shapes between the lines. The greatest possibility for this sort of linear construction is offered with wire; therefore, it will be treated separately in the next chapter. Wire sculpture may be said to bear the same relationship to construction that drawing does to painting.

Construction (9" high) by Bob, grade 3; New Lincoln School, New York.

Construction (5" high) by Herman, grade 9; Rye High School, Rye, New York.

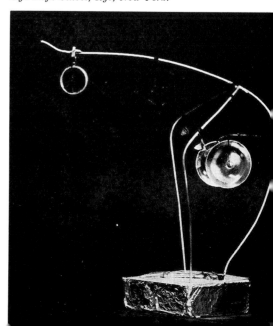

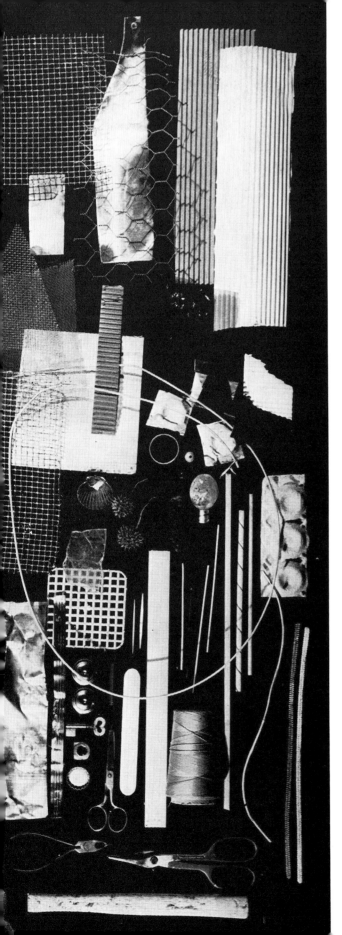

materials for construction

It is important to provide a variety of provocative materials for construction. Many suggested for collage can also be used for construction. Teachers and students who keep searching will find an increasing number of inspiring materials which offer possibilities of being used together.

Some materials, such as those mentioned here, are resistant or hard. Scrap wood in different sizes and shapes is usually available from the school shop or a lumber yard. Tongue depressors and swab sticks can be bought in large boxes at drugstores. Ice-cream or lollipop sticks and toothpicks are also useful. Colored sticks in eight-inch lengths, made for kindergarten use, can be ordered from school supply houses. Balsa wood in thin sticks and thick chunks is useful, especially in junior high school, as are wood dowels in quarter- and half-inch diameters. Another resistant material is stiff cardboard that will not bend. From it shapes can be cut to be used in a construction or it can be combined with other materials; and laminated cardboard with a corrugated ply in the center has many uses in construction.

Flexible materials should also be available. All the wires described on Page 74 can be combined with other materials. Basket reed is adaptable and plastic tubing called "spaghetti" costs little and comes in a variety of colors and diameters from electrical supply houses.

Flexible papers include construction paper, heavy drawing paper and tagboard. Many thin cardboards can be salvaged, such as shirt boards, thin cartons or old playing cards. Thin illustration board is good for junior high school students. Flexible colored corrugated cardboard can be bought or found in scrap.

Metals may be used in many ways in constructions and introduce a different kind of surface. Kitchen aluminum foil is easy for young children to handle. Older children can manage thin sheet metal, like copper. Less expensive than copper is thin aluminum flashing which can be cut with scissors and is obtainable from building supply houses. Junior high school students can use metal from tin cans.

Transparent materials have particular value in the making of constructions. In addition to cellophane and gelatin, thin colored plastics can be used. Glass is suitable for junior high school students and bits of glass collected from the seashore are particularly good, as are scraps of plastic of varying thicknesses. Discarded strip film is also usable.

All sorts of wire screening are excellent for constructions, including plastic fly screening which is easy to work and does not cut or scratch. Sometimes hardware stores are willing to save scraps for a local school.

Colored string and colored wool are useful to have on hand. For junior high school students, black thread should be provided for suspending objects on mobiles when they want the string to be invisible.

Small objects which are usable include corks, flash-bulbs, bottle tops and a variety of bolts, washers and other hardware articles.

Some kinds of constructions can be built by combining and modifying ready-made forms. Boxes, ranging up in size from match boxes, and cardboard tubes in all diameters can be brought in by students. Paper drinking cups, both conical and cylindrical, can be used by children of all ages.

Scrap cardboard is improved if painted different colors. Painting cardboard for future use makes a good job for students who finish their own work before the end of a period.

Essential tools for making constructions are scissors, cutting pliers and a hammer. Additional tools which are desirable but not essential include serrated kitchen shears, which are efficient for cutting cardboard, a stapler and paper punch.

Students in junior high school will find additional tools useful; for example, metal shears, a hand or electric drill, an electric soldering iron and a knife.

For hanging constructions or mobiles, a string should be suspended for each child. It can be tied to a paper clip which is easy to hook to a wire or heavy string extended across the classroom. If a loop is tied near the bottom of each child's string, the mobile can be raised when he has finished working, as illustrated below. In some schools it is possible to extend wires permanently across the room; in others a heavy string can be put up temporarily the day children are working on mobiles. Some art rooms have rods extending across the room that can be raised and lowered by ropes run through pulleys attached to the walls. When this is the case the whole rod is lowered for pupils to work and their mobiles can be made on short strings.

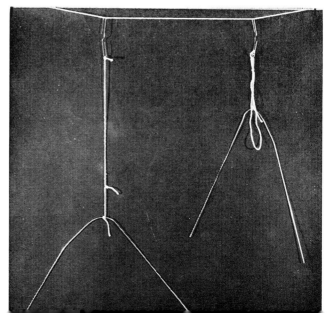

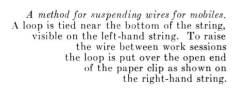

A method for suspending wires for mobiles. A loop is tied near the bottom of the string, visible on the left-hand string. To raise the wire between work sessions the loop is put over the open end of the paper clip as shown on the right-hand string.

suggestions for the teacher

The teacher who understands what boys and girls will gain from the experience, as suggested previously, can best help them explore fully the possibilities of working with three-dimensional materials.

In collage, the teacher's emphasis should be on the visual and tactile quality of the materials and how sensitively they can be arranged on a flat surface. In construction, the emphasis is on the structural quality of the materials and how they can be joined to make a three-dimensional design in which materials and open-space shapes are related.

Consideration of what the children can learn will help the teacher in collecting materials for constructions. For example, if only sticks and feathers were given to a group of young children there would be few possibilities beyond sticking them into a clay base. If some materials that bend, like wire or corrugated cardboard strips, were added the possibilities for design and structure would be greatly increased.

Some materials in themselves suggest possibilities of how they may best be put together. For example, straws, beads, corrugated cardboard or mesh made of cloth or wire, have holes; others, like paper or thin metal, will bend. It is important also to offer a variety of colors and textures in the materials.

It is particularly important in making hanging constructions to stress arrangement and offer materials which can be joined in different ways. Unless attention is given to this, the making of mobiles can degenerate into a meaningless activity in which objects are merely suspended from a piece of wire or coat hanger.

Materials themselves, as has already been mentioned, often suggest the main inspiration in making constructions. To help boys and girls become involved in what they are making, the teacher gives them the opportunity at the beginning of class to look at and feel the materials and to discuss the possibilities of using them in three-dimensional designs.

A teacher can often help a pupil be more inventive by giving a provocative hint when he needs it. Here is one example: Laura, who was six, asked for some sticky tape to attach a piece of corrugated cardboard to a stick on her construction. Transparent tape had not been provided because children can become so dependent on it that they do not devise other ways of joining, so the teacher said, "Laura, there are better ways of joining. Here is a piece of wire. Does it give you any ideas?" Laura took the wire and said, "Oh, I can put it through this hole." The teacher then said, "Good, can you find another way, too?" Laura worked on, and soon called excitedly, "I have invented three ways altogether." She then decided not to use the wire but to put the stick already on her construction through the hole in the cardboard. Had the teacher told her of this solution in the beginning, instead of giving her a hint towards finding her own ways, Laura would have been deprived of the growth in her development that came from independently reaching the right solution for her design.

A teacher helps also by comments to a pupil about his work. He may discuss or praise the child's selection of materials and the shapes he has built with them or he may mention the way materials have been joined. This can help the pupil go on learning and inventing further ways to construct. By mentioning qualities of design and originality the pupil has intuitively achieved, the teacher will help him toward further growth and understanding of three-dimensional design.

Construction (4" high) by Lucas, 3 years,
Bank Street School, New York.
To the wire stapled to a base, Lucas added a piece of
styrofoam and a thin wire. Then he looped and
twisted the wire adding another piece of styrofoam
and toothpicks.

construction
in preschool
and kindergarten

Photos in this section by Lois Lord.

It is natural for very young children to work
with three-dimensional materials and when
they do so their involvement is often intense.
They delight in arranging objects in various
combinations and they will experimentally
bend and manipulate materials that are pliable.

In nursery school and kindergarten boys and
girls learn to explore space-form relationships
as they build with blocks. In addition, further
opportunities should be offered for working
with a variety of three-dimensional materials,
both flexible and resisting.

Flexible materials could include soft wire
cut in small lengths, pipe cleaners, strips of
colored corrugated cardboard. Small objects
that could be attached to these might also be
provided, such as small buttons, toothpicks,
colored sticks, bits of styrofoam. With materials like these, young children usually need
a base upon which to start their constructions,
such as a small lump of plasticine, clay, salt-
flour dough or a piece of styrofoam, or the
teacher could staple a piece of wire to a cardboard or wooden base for each child (as in the
construction made by Lucas, above).

In introducing construction, a teacher might
first give each child a piece of soft wire and one

other material like a strip of corrugated or a
piece of styrofoam or a small object with which
to experiment so that he can explore the possibilities of bending and joining.

The combination of materials set out by the
teacher should be varied successively as the
children gain experience. They need experiences making both large and small constructions. By five years, most children can manage
to use wire itself as the base and it becomes
a challenge to make it stand up. Joe made
his construction (page 46) by carefully attaching
more wire and corrugated strips to the wire he
had first bent. However, some base should be
provided for those who prefer it.

Constructing with wood offers limitless possibilities for the young child. Scrap wood is
easily obtainable and the variety of shapes
provides the young child with the opportunity

Construction (16" high) by Lisa, 3½ years,
Bank Street School, New York.
Lisa carefully counted as she put three bits of plastic
tubing on the wire alternating them between each
piece of styrofoam. She found there was space only
for one at the top.

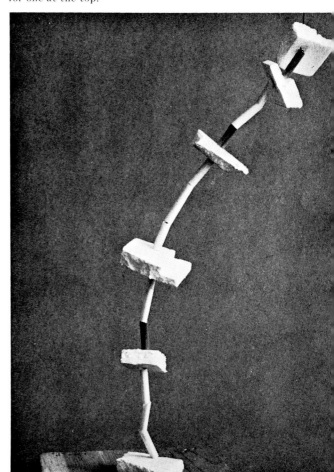

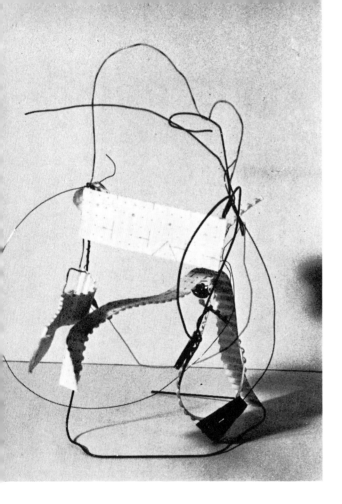

Construction (8″ high) by Joe, 5 years,
New Lincoln School, New York.
Joe bent a wire so it would stand up and then
added pieces of fine wire and strips of corrugated
cardboard and buttons to make this interesting
three-dimensional design.

of making choices as he builds his piece. With
the wood, small objects may be offered, such
as: spools, corks, bottle tops. Three- and
four-year-olds may experiment with making
many arrangements with these materials before
glue is given to them. The teacher should
comment at the same time on the arrangement and the way in which the pieces are
constructed, as both learnings are important
for the young child.

After a child has learned to glue he can
usually learn to hammer nails. At first the
construction may be nothing more than nails
hammered into wood, usually in some kind of
arrangement. Most children use nails both
structurally and decoratively in their wood
constructions.

Small boxes and objects combined can inspire young children to make interesting constructions. Peter chose spools and plastic
pill boxes to make an original construction.
The relationships are interesting because Peter
achieved contrast by choosing transparent and
solid cylinders and by arranging them at
different heights.

Small rectangular boxes in a variety of sizes
may also be given to children either separately
or to combine with cylinders. Shoe or other
box covers or pieces of cardboard can be used
for a base on which to glue or arrange them.
As soon as three-year-olds have learned to
paste paper they will be able to glue wood,
cardboard and other materials.

All of these kinds of constructions offer
young children challenge in mastery of skills
as well as in thinking and forming three-
dimensional relationships. Motivation will
come from the way the teacher offers successively different combinations of materials.
The teacher can reinforce learning by commenting on any sensitive or inventive decision
a child has made.

Construction (10″ high) by Peter, 4½ years.
Peter made an arrangement of solid
and transparent cylinders by gluing
together spools and pillboxes.

Construction (15″ long) by Paul, 4 years, Bank Street School, New York.
Paul made a subtle arrangement of levels in the way he placed corks on the
wooden base he built up with pieces of wood.

Bank Street School, New York. Sheri, 5 years, quickly
adds another piece of wood to her construction. She
had made a strong design around the triangular piece
of wood she placed near the center of the base. She
used both glue and nails.

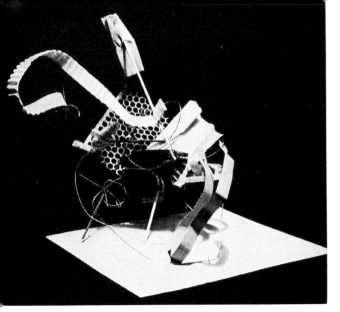

Construction (8" high) by Susan; Center School, New Canaan, Connecticut; Susan started with a wire stapled to cardboard, then joined to it paper, cardboard and plastic mesh.

construction in grades one and two

Children delight in the quality and color of materials. Therefore, when six- and seven-year-olds are to make constructions they should choose from a variety of materials which have visual appeal and also provide many possibilities for being attached one to another. A first selection of materials offered should include some that are flexible, such as pipe cleaners, florist's wire, strips of corrugated cardboard and strips of paper. These will contrast with stiff objects like toothpicks, sticks, drinking straws and bits of stiff cardboard, plain and corrugated.

Astronaut in his Capsule (12" high) by Henry, grade 1, New Lincoln School, New York. Henry organized the inside space of the capsule by the way he placed the astronaut and by the way he glued varying lengths of dowel to the interior wall.

The teacher may introduce the materials with a short discussion: "Look at these materials, find out what they are like. Which can you bend or fold?" Young children investigate materials with their hands and eyes. The teacher suggests, "Choose some materials to make a three-dimensional design. Can you find ways of joining the materials to make new shapes?" Children's constructions can be as diverse and individual as their work in paint, clay and other media.

Some children, without previous experience, may want, at first, to use a piece of everything that has been put out by the teacher. Such a beginning is typical of some children. Later, the teacher will encourage them to select a few materials and to use them with greater discrimination.

Susan had had some experience with constructions when she made the example illustrated above. She chose a few materials from many and intuitively created a unified design.

It is wise for the teacher to prepare ahead of time for a session in making hanging constructions. For each child in the group she can hang up a string to which she has tied a piece of wire, a pipe cleaner or a strip of corrugated cardboard. The teacher might introduce hanging constructions thus: "When you make a design that hangs, you will want to think of how it will look as it turns and moves. As you work you will find ways to attach the materials so they will not fall off."

The first spontaneous hanging construction is usually an expression of the child's delight in the materials. Often he will take a little of each material and attach it to his hanging wire. With experience he will learn more about the materials, become more selective and begin to give care to the organization of shapes.

Geoffrey's construction, right, shows that he has had experience and a sensitive approach to materials. He worked for several art periods on this and was expressing his idea of an imaginary radar station. Each object and

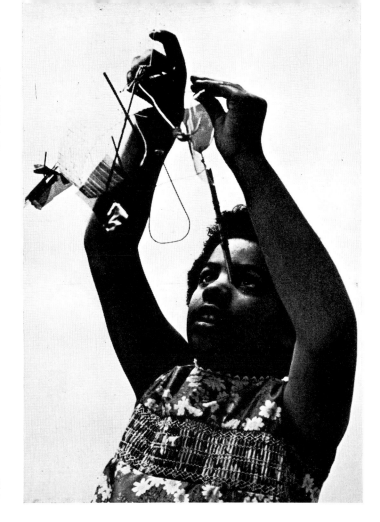

Moira, grade 2,
New Lincoln School, New York.
Moira is involved in
solving problems in design
and construction as she
works on her hanging
construction.

Photo: Lois Lord

Radar Station (18″ long) by Geoffrey,
grade 2; New Lincoln School, New York.
Scraps of wood, wire mesh, fine sticks and
odd bits of metal were chosen by Geoffrey
and put together with hammer and nails
in a well-organized and creative way.

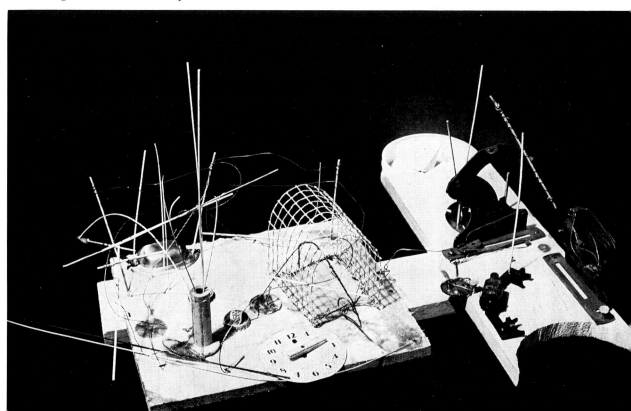

*Construction (14" high), by Rachel, grade 1,
New Lincoln School, New York.*
Rachel arranged and glued pre-cut pieces
of wood to make this construction
in which verticals and horizontals
together form a unified design.

To make constructions with wood is highly challenging to six- and seven-year-olds. Children can be given the opportunity to experiment with space-form relationships if they are provided with pre-cut pieces to assemble. Then, if they are given support from the teacher they will grow in understanding and the ability to create three-dimensional organization. For example, the teacher might say to Steve about his construction (below), "You have built two towers differently. On the near one you have built triangles on top of one another so there is an opening down the center. The other has solid pieces in the center and openings at the sides. You have arranged them together so that the wood and the spaces in between make an interesting design."

At first glance Steve's construction may appear less advanced than Rachel's (above). The structural order is less apparent because Steve is working with a greater variety of elements and he has created in one piece a greater variety of order.

On each successive occasion that a group makes constructions the teacher may say a little more about arranging materials to make a three-dimensional design. For stimulation, new materials can be added or different combinations offered. The aim is always to give children an opportunity to grow in their ability to select, invent and design in space.

joint contributes to a complicated story of messages going in and out. Some of the metal bits can be moved up and down, establishing a variety of connections.

*Construction (15" long) by Steve,
grade 2, New Lincoln School,
New York.*
Steve made a complex
organization of solids
and voids by building
two towers, one with an open
and one with a solid core.
He has related the
elements in an organized design.

Hanging Construction (14" wide) by Paul, grade 3; New Lincoln School, New York. To a strip of corrugated cardboard suspended on a string Paul attached wires and sticks. He added more cardboard and sticks each of which has a function as well as an interesting visual relationship.

construction in grades three and four

Children of eight or nine seem to have a high sense of three-dimensional organization and love to make constructions. They work spontaneously but are able to plan more thoughtfully and are more skillful than younger children. Materials are a direct motivation for them and little discussion seems necessary at the beginning of a class. This makes it extremely important that the materials be set out so boys and girls have ample opportunity to examine and select from them.

Wood might be provided for bases, along with hammer and staples. Bases can also be made of heavy cardboard, with wires poked through or stapled with a paper stapler, or attached with paper fasteners. Styrofoam can be available for those who prefer it.

If third- and fourth-graders have not made constructions they should be encouraged to explore and experiment as was suggested for younger children. A child's development is stimulated when a teacher comments on his particular selection, arrangement or invention in his construction.

As children gain experience and confidence, the teacher could encourage more thoughtful selection by saying, "Look at these materials and decide whether you would like to choose some of them for a construction that stands or one that hangs."

As children become even more experienced they can be encouraged, on some occasions, to work with fewer materials in order to find new possibilities in each of them. For example, flexible cardboard can be bent and joined to

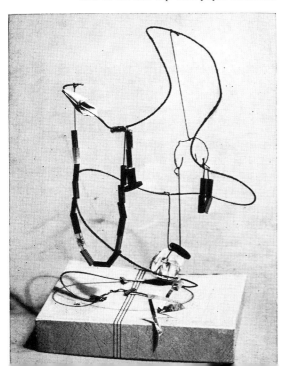

Construction (7" high) by Melody, grade 4; River Road School, Mount Pleasant, Delaware. With wire, glass beads and buttons, hanging some parts with string so they will move, Melody has created a rhythmic three-dimensional design. She attached the wire to the box top with paper fasteners.

51

Cardboard Construction (11″ high) by Ellen, grade 4; Midtown Ethical Culture School, New York.
A complex construction in which one piece of cardboard is folded, bent and joined
and other pieces are added to it by slitting. Ellen incorporated texture by
using cardboard from an egg crate and other collage materials.

itself with staples or toothpicks. Stiff cardboard can be joined by cutting a slit in each piece. One teacher suggested, "Make your main shapes with cardboard and then see what other materials you would like to add to give variety in the other shapes."

Cardboard is the basic material in Ellen's construction, above. It is not only richly decorated on all sides but she has made a closed shape penetrated by straight pieces of cardboard. The children in this group had been collecting materials for weeks, thus becoming aware of the possibilities in using them.

Dove (7″ long) by Mardell, grade 3; Lapham School, Madison, Wisconsin. Mardell has skillfully put together boxes and cardboard tubes to suggest his idea of a dove.

Photo: University of Wisconsin Photographic Laboratory

Another way of constructing is using cardboard boxes and tubes. This kind of construction can be abstract or it may express an idea, as Mardell did in his *Dove*, left.

Scrap metal can be combined in a variety of ways with other materials to make abstract constructions or symbolizations. Donald and Rosemary, whose constructions are to the right, selected carefully from many materials. In this case the teacher suggested "animals." She provided enough different objects to inspire each child to transform them into symbols in an original way. Rosemary used a paper cup for her lion's head while Donald used an angle iron to suggest a head.

Paper is a material which can be used by itself in many ways, both for stabiles and hanging constructions. Paper, white or colored, can be bent, folded or curved and attached with paste, stapler or by making slits in itself. At first the children should have plenty of time to experiment so they will have more means at their disposal when making a finished design.

Rocket for Putting out Fires (8″ high)
by Steven, grade 3,
New Lincoln School, New York.
Steven was thoughtful as he worked
carefully with wire, sticks and
cardboard tube to make this
imaginary rocket.

Animal (4″ high) by Donald
and Lion (7″ high)
by Rosemary, 10 years;
Bank Street School, New York.
Materials for these animals
were imaginatively chosen
from many scrap materials.
Donald added metal, wire,
screws and bolts to a
can to make his fantastic
animal. Rosemary chose
wood, metal, a paper cup, fur
and rice to create this
original symbol of a lion.

Animals (9" high) by Chip, grade 5; New Lincoln School, New York. Chip chose materials with discrimination and imagination and put them together ingeniously to create these animals, He used wires, sheet aluminum and fine and coarse wire mesh.

construction in grades five and six

By fifth and sixth grades children use three-dimensional materials to express feelings, experiences or fantasies. Some, of course, will prefer always to build abstract structures and others will use the materials to suggest a subject.

Children who have not previously worked with these materials may be timid about starting because at this age they often work more thoughtfully and some of them feel the need to know some possibilities before exploring for themselves. Though the same approach mentioned for younger children should be used, more motivation may be necessary. First, the children must be inspired by the materials. The teacher might say, "How many ways could you fold or bend a strip of paper or a length of wire to make it three-dimensional?" or, "How could you join several of these materials to make them stand up?" After a short discussion about the materials the teacher could suggest, "Choose some of these materials to make a beautiful design in which each small part relates to the whole. Some of you may wish to make a design about something you know or imagine."

Construction (12" high) by Matthew, 10 years; Museum of Modern Art Classes, New York. In this subtle arrangement the linear shapes Matthew made from wire and cellophane straws are echoed by the conical paper cups.

Children who have previously had a rich experience with these materials will attain further growth by more conscious organization for expression and design. It may add challenge to introduce more difficult materials like thin metals and all sorts of wire mesh.

Fifth- and sixth-graders are able to plan their constructions more thoughtfully than do younger children. As their knowledge of materials increases they often seek out or ask for some particular thing they' need. Some children select a few from many available materials, as Matthew did for his construction at bottom of facing page. Others, like Barry, whose construction is on Page 57, choose to organize many materials. At times, some children may prefer to construct with one material as shown by the toothpick and stick constructions, right. This kind of material demands painstaking work which some children enjoy, but is tiresome for others.

Toothpick Constructions (10″ high) by Carol and Linda, grade 5; North Bennington Graded School, Vermont. Bright colored toothpicks were joined with plastic cement to make these dynamic constructions.

Grasshopper (9″ high) by Larry, grade 5; New Lincoln School, New York. Larry used fine wire to join sticks in constructing his highly original concept of a grasshopper.

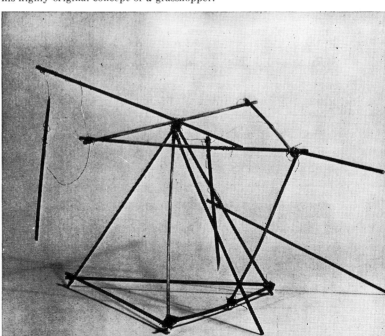

Circus (48" long) by Mary, grade 6; Midtown Ethical Culture School, New York. Mary used aluminum foil for the animals and then built up the circus with reed, tongue depressors, wires and chicken wire. She has expressed, with spirit, much that goes on in a circus.

Other materials suitable to use alone for constructions are paper, cardboard, thin metals or metal screening. The aim is always to give children the opportunity to know materials and to make personal choices. Larry, who was familiar with many materials, had been to the circus. He came to class with an idea and got out the materials he wanted for his hanging circus construction, illustrated at top of facing page. Last of all he hung strips of yellow and blue cellophane around the edge, "To give it the gay feeling of a circus," he said.

Mary, on the other hand, was hesitant with all art media. She said she had been to the circus but could not paint it. The teacher suggested that she make some animals from aluminum foil. After making the animals she used other materials, taking several art periods to build her circus, above. It was admired by her classmates and thus her status with the group improved and her self-confidence began to appear. In addition, the satisfaction she derived from this achievement helped her attitude toward painting.

At times a teacher could give a subject-oriented motivation such as, "How can you combine these materials to suggest an animal?" or, "Imaginary people" or "Space men" or "A city of the future," or "A group of people."

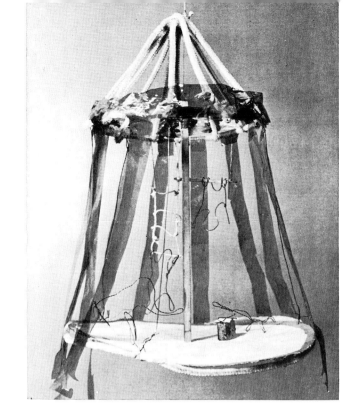

Circus (14″ high) by Larry, grade 5; New Lincoln School, New York. To make this hanging construction of a circus ring Larry chose cardboard, pipe cleaners and a balsa wood stick. Wire figures swing on string trapezes and blue and yellow cellophane strips were added at the end.

Construction (20″ high) by Barry, grade 6; Midtown Ethical Culture School, New York. In this sensitively organized construction Barry started with a cardboard cone and then attached sticks, strips of cardboard and string. He repeated the main shape by making two small cones of paper. He decorated the base and part of the cone with collage materials.

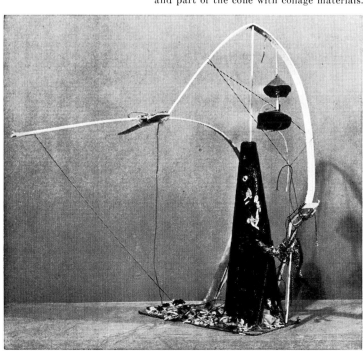

Photo: Morris Rosenfeld

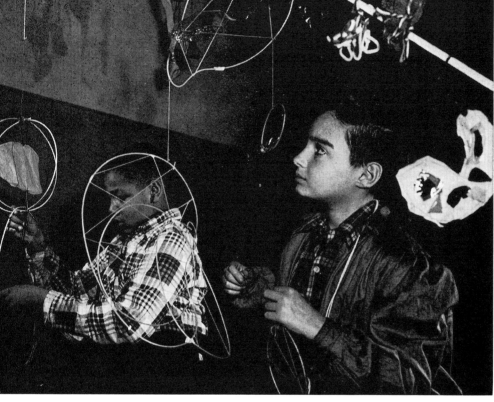

Sixth-graders making Mobiles; Midtown Ethical Culture School, New York.
Both these boys are using reed, paper and string. Sammy, *left,* is working on a simple circular form in which he placed his paper fish. Robert, *right,* is concentrating on ways to balance a new part on his complex abstract mobile which has several moving parts.

Fifth- and sixth-graders should be encouraged to make various kinds of hanging constructions. Robert, on the right in the picture above, used several materials for his non-representational construction. Susan's, facing page, top, is different for she wanted to give the feeling of fish moving within the linear shape she made with wire. She hung fish on different lengths of string so they could swing as the mobile turned. To children of this age it could be pointed out that objects will swing if they are hung on a single, not a double, length of string.

As children work, they can be encouraged to think about problems of balance and motion, thereby learning greater control of their designs. The teacher might ask, "Your design is made to hang. How can you construct it so it will move? Do you want to make parts that will move separately?"

The problem of the difference between physi-cal and visual balance is important. One sixth-grader discovered it and said, "I thought this piece of metal could make my mobile balance. It looks right but is too light." The teacher pointed out that either he could cut a heavier material to the same size or adjust the weight of material on the opposite side.

At one school, fifth-graders became so anxious to get a variety of movement in their mobiles that they took up in science class the study of balance. The knowledge gained helped them know how to make their mobiles look and balance as they wished.

Some children of this age may become so interested in three-dimensional work that they will want to continue with it while their classmates go on to other media. In such cases the teacher should provide opportunities for each child to grow and become more skillful and imaginative in his way of working.

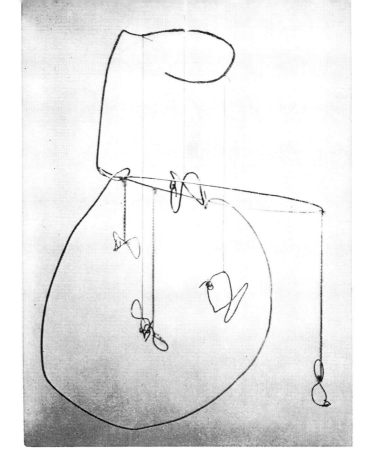

Fish Bowl (15" high) by Susan, grade 6; New Lincoln School, New York. In this mobile the wire fish, suspended on red and black strings, move freely within the interesting wire shapes that suggest the bowl.

Yellow Bug by Nancy, grade 6; Herbert Schenk School, Madison, Wisconsin. Nancy put together shapes for the body and head, skillfully adding bits of pot cleaners for wings and head decoration.

Baseball Player (8" long) by Carol Ann, grade 6; New Lincoln School, New York. Carol Ann put together sticks, wire, cellophane and paper in such a way that the whole figure moves. The shoulders swing up and down and the hands revolve on their string arms.

Destruction from Outer Space (12″ high) by Carlisle, grade 8; Rye High School, Rye, New York. Carlisle selected materials with discrimination to express his idea. He built the delicate skeleton structure with sticks and modeled the small figures from wax. In contrast, the large figure of a space man is made of wood and wire with a spool for the head.

Construction (8″ high) by Donna, 12 years; Museum of Modern Art Classes, New York. The circle made of pipe cleaners softly contrasts in color, texture and shape with the angular forms which penetrate it. This sensitive arrangement is enhanced by the transparent straws put over the wires.

Students will learn to make increasingly discriminating choices. To guide them, the teacher might ask, "Does this shape look right in relation to the whole design?" or, "How can you make this shape look as well-related from the back as it does from the side?"

Donna and Paul had not made constructions before. From the materials set out each selected a few to make a different kind of construction. Donna chose to make an abstract linear design of open space shapes which she related in a sensitive way, illustrated left. Paul's construction, below, is different from Donna's not only because the materials suggested to him a representational subject but

Knight (14" high) by Paul, 12 years; Museum of Modern Art Classes, New York. The cardboard bottle cover suggested a knight to Paul who then chose wire, straws, moss and gelatin to carry out his idea.

construction in junior high school

Both girls and boys in junior high school enjoy three-dimensional work. If during elementary school years they have had challenging experiences with three-dimensional materials, continued work with them offers the opportunity to study the principles of three-dimensional design on a more mature and conscious level. If they have not had experience, the materials offered for constructions may inspire them to work with more spirit and spontaneity than they often are able to bring to more traditional materials.

Some junior high school students, like Donna, whose construction is above, choose to work abstractly. Others, like Carlisle, use materials to express ideas, Page 60. As they gain experience students work with more conscious thought and planning. They like to feel they are learning as they create. Making constructions can give students a sense of mastery over many different materials and the techniques necessary to use them.

Wood Construction (12" high)
by Richard, grade 8; Laurel Special
School District, Delaware.
Richard used imagination in seeing
possibilities in available materials for
making this unusual wood construction.
He placed thumbtacks in a pattern
and strung from them bits of
metal and wood. The painted
decoration on the base adds a rich
contrast to the natural texture
of the wood above.

also because he used a closed form for his main
shape. The addition of contrasting materials
makes an interesting design and expresses his
imaginative idea.

The teacher can inspire enthusiasm so that
students will work thoughtfully and continue to
approach materials with spontaneity and sensitivity. A teacher generates enthusiasm in
several ways: the way he sets out materials,
the way in which he conducts the discussion
and his encouragement of originality. By
eighth grade, some students are often able to
work for several periods on one construction,
striving for design and careful workmanship.
These qualities are apparent in the construction, *Destruction from Outer Space*, Page 60,
made by Carlisle who was experienced in using
three-dimensional materials.

At times, students who have made constructions combining a number of materials should
be encouraged to construct with only one or

two at a time. Thus, they have the opportunity to gain more depth of knowledge of the
possibilities inherent in each.

A series of problems might include such
different kinds of constructions as those in
which emphasis is on the relationship of the
shapes of the materials used, as in the paper
constructions on Pages 66 and 67, or those in
which emphasis is on the spaces between the
materials or on the linear quality, as in Peter's
construction, facing page.

Seventh- and eighth-grade students gradually develop conscious understanding of space-
form relationships as a result of their own
efforts and the comments the teacher makes to
them about their work.

By ninth grade, experienced students are
usually ready for and can become interested in
more discussion and theory before they begin
to work. Many are capable of grasping, on
progressive levels of thought, deeper concepts

of space relationships in three-dimensional design. The teacher might discuss with them: What is a space-shape created by materials? For example, he might ask, "What is the shape of the space made by cupping the hands? How is this shape changed as one moves the hands farther apart? What is the actual space-shape of a room? If one joins the two ends of a strip of paper, what space-shape does it make?" Such discussions can be related to a variety of different materials at different times. The teacher will be guided in how far to carry analysis of principles by the interest and intellectual capacity of the group. Some students will always work more intuitively and will therefore profit less than others from theoretical discussions. This group will likely gain most from detailed analysis by the teacher of the constructions they have already made.

The imagination of ninth-grade students is often stimulated by facing art problems within limitations. The teacher may present a problem using only one material or suggest some limitation in the way students may work with a given material.

Constructions which are essentially linear may be made with materials like sticks, balsa

Construction (17″ high) by Peter, grade 8; Fieldston School, New York. In this linear construction the large volumes made by curved lines of reed have been broken by straight lines of bright colored wools.

Head with Loose Screws (11" high) by Eddie, grade 9; Baron Byng High School, Montreal, Canada. Eddie used balsa wood sticks to indicate the planes in this original and dramatic abstraction of a head. He covered the eyes and nose with cellophane and suspended bits of metal and wire on strings for the loose screws.

wood, reed or wire. These may be used alone, in combination with each other, or combined with transparent materials like net or cellophane. Ellen's construction was the result of a problem in which the students were asked to create a three-dimensional design using only horizontal and vertical lines. The aim was to create a design with thick and thin lines and open areas of related space-shapes. Using transparent net or cellophane to make divisions in the space gave the students opportunity to relate the smaller divisions of space to the whole design. This kind of problem can help students become more sensitive to space relationships in modern architecture.

Eddie used balsa wood sticks, placed in several different directions, for the head, illustrated above. Thick balsa wood may be carved and glued to make interesting constructions, as in George's, bottom of facing page.

*Construction (9″ high) by Ellen,
grade 9; New Lincoln School, New York.*
In this architectural construction
Ellen has created a series of
well related straight line volumes using
balsa wood sticks in varying widths.
Supports are effectively planned as
part of the design and a subtle use of
translucent and transparent surfaces
emphasizes certain areas.

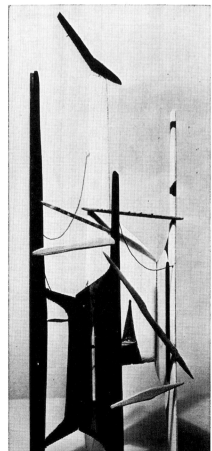

*Wood Construction (12″ high) by George, grade 9; High School
of Music and Art, New York.* George carved balsa wood into
delicate shapes which he glued together to make this
carefully thought out design. He added a few curved
wire lines and decoratively painted the construction
in tones of black, white and gray.

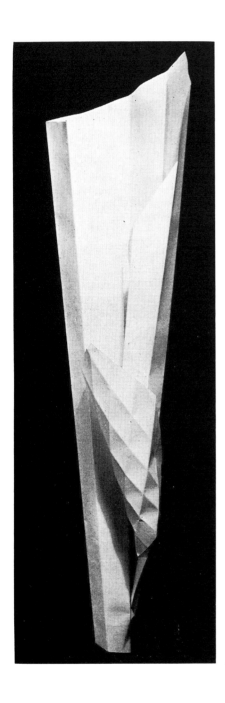

Paper Constructions (18" and 9" high) by Miriam and Lila, grade 9; New Lincoln School, New York. Two different solutions to the problem of creating a construction by bending and folding a sheet of paper without cutting anything away. Miriam scored and fluted her paper while Lila rolled and curled hers before joining.

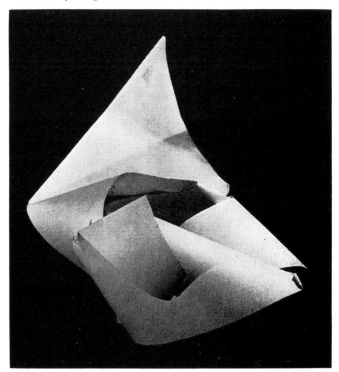

Different weights of paper offer many possibilities for construction. Working with paper, which is flat, helps students comprehend the ways in which a flat material can be used to make a three-dimensional form. Constructions may be made by bending strips of paper or, like those above, by cutting into a sheet and bending it without cutting anything away. This particular problem was intriguing to a large group. After class one child said, "Let's have that problem again next week, there is so much to it." Another added, "Wouldn't it be great to make decorations like that for a dance."

Other problems can involve constructing with shapes cut from cardboard or heavy paper and joining them by making slits in themselves. One such problem might result in a composition which was open, or it could result in a composition in which the spaces were

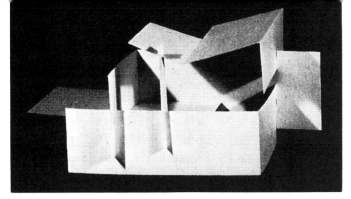

The House by Tommy, grade 9;
Rye High School, Rye, New York. This construction
was built by slitting and joining pieces of cardboard.
Tommy scored and folded cardboard before joining it.

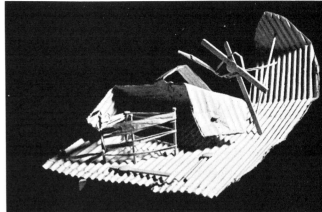

Construction (12" long) by Ann, grade 9,
New Lincoln School, New York.
After bending the cardboard and adding sticks,
nails and string, Ann sprayed her
construction white. She then placed
it in the light so that the
values and colors in the shadows
were most interesting.

Construction (14" long) by John, grade 9,
New Lincoln School, New York.
In this construction chipboard was
carefully cut and glued and the
simple strength of space-form
relationships is emphasized by
painting part black and part white.

enclosed. This problem could be varied by
offering a number of colored cardboards from
which to choose and combine, thus adding the
dimension of the organization of colored surfaces in space. Some students like to work in
large scale, while others prefer to work small.

Tommy's *Building*, above, was one solution
to a problem of constructing by cutting and
folding, then joining, paper. Other students in
the group used the same technique to make
abstract designs. John's construction, right,
was made by cutting heavy chipboard and
gluing it together.

Thin metal can be used in ways similar to
paper. It may be used alone or combined with
wire mesh or other materials, as illustrated by
the constructions on Page 68.

Making constructions with transparent pieces
of glass or plexiglass gives students a chance
to make three-dimensional designs in which
all parts can simultaneously be seen through
the transparent planes and hence the unity

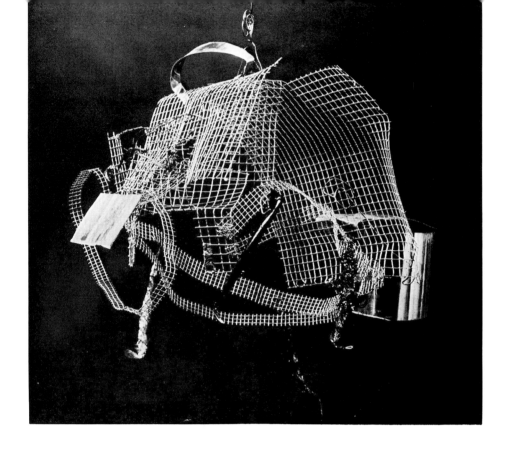

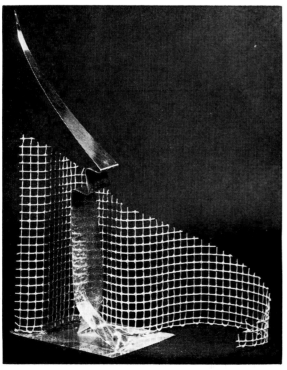

Imaginary Animal: above (24″ long), by John, grade 8; New Lincoln School, New York. John worked seriously to carry out his humorous idea for which he chose metal and wire mesh. *Dancer, left (11″ high), by Timothy, grade 9; Rye High School, Rye, New York.* Timothy cut three simple shapes of metal and wire mesh to make this sensitive abstract dancer. The delicacy of the central shape is enhanced by reflections in it. These two boys, equally skilled and imaginative, worked very differently; John's style is bold and complex while Timothy's is refined and simple.

Glass Constructions by John and Ralph, grade 9; Rye High School, Rye, New York. Clear and colored glass was cemented together to make these unusual constructions.

Mobile (9" high) by Janice, grade 7; Rye High School, Rye, New York. Janice suspended bits of colored glass from a heavy wire she had bent and attached to a cork base.

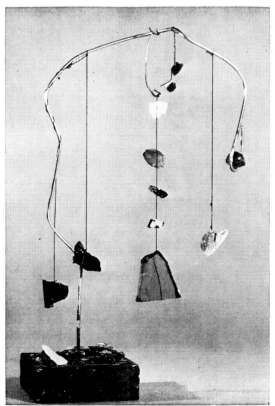

of the whole can be perceived at all times from any angle. If glass or plastic is used, it might be suggested that the first two pieces be cemented together at right angles with plastic cement so they will stand up. After the first two pieces have dried overnight, any number of pieces can be added.

Most junior high school students are fascinated with making mobiles. If they have not made them before, students may start by making hanging constructions, as suggested for younger children. By junior high school age most students are able to work out problems of balance and motion. The teacher can indicate that some parts of a mobile may be planned in fixed positions, while others turn. The student

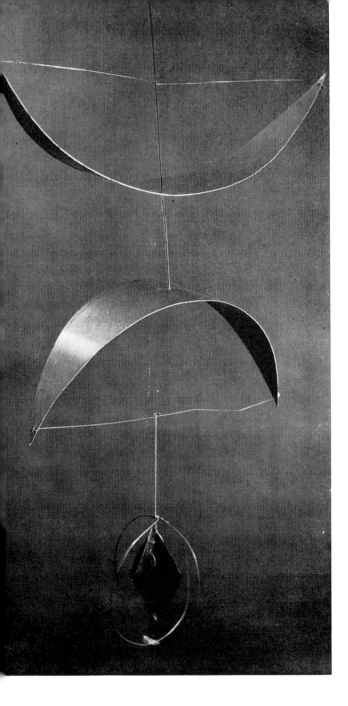

Mobile (14" wide) by Judy, grade 7; North Junior High School, Great Neck, New York. Judy designed and cut simple shapes from aluminum flashing, connecting them with wire. She used string to suspend the lowest form so it would move.

must try to make the actual movement an integral part of the design. The teacher can further indicate ways to control both motion and balance. To control balance, the fulcrum can be changed or weight can be added or subtracted from one side to the other, as in a seesaw. While Judy was making her mobile, left, the teacher asked whether she wanted to suspend the two large metal shapes with string instead of wire so they could move in opposite directions. Judy said, "No, I want them always to turn together as they are now and I want only the lowest shape to turn in different directions." The teacher's question made Judy aware that she was sensitively planning her design by contrasting a moving part to two fixed shapes.

Sometimes there is the added factor, in making mobiles, of the shadow cast on the wall from the mobile and its relationship in motion to the mobile itself. Colored glass and cellophane cast colored shadows.

The interest in some mobiles is in the organization of many suspended shapes. Such mobiles may hang from the ceiling or be attached to a stand, like the one on Page 69, by Janice. Here the teacher stressed the relationship of the sizes of objects and the heights from which they were suspended.

As students become experienced, they can make mobiles which are more refined and complex in the relationship of parts. This is demonstrated in the mobiles of Wayne and Tom, illustrated on the facing page.

Right: —→

Planets (15" high) by Tom, grade 8; Rye High School, Rye, New York. In this mobile subtle balance and motion were achieved by delicately adjusting the position and weights of the globes made of wire.

Wayne making a mobile, grade 9; Van Horn High School, Kansas City, Missouri. Wayne created interesting forms from shapes he cut from wood and cardboard, suspending them one within another. He is working out the design and balance by hanging them from rods.

Photo: Art Department, Public Schools, Kansas City, Missouri.

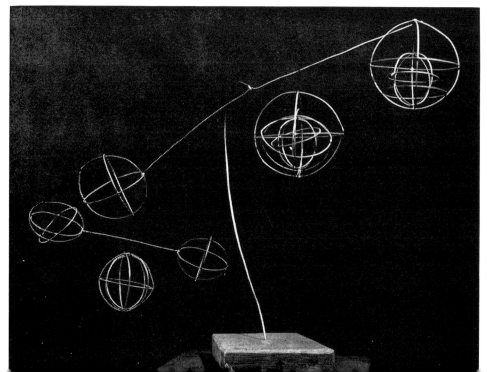

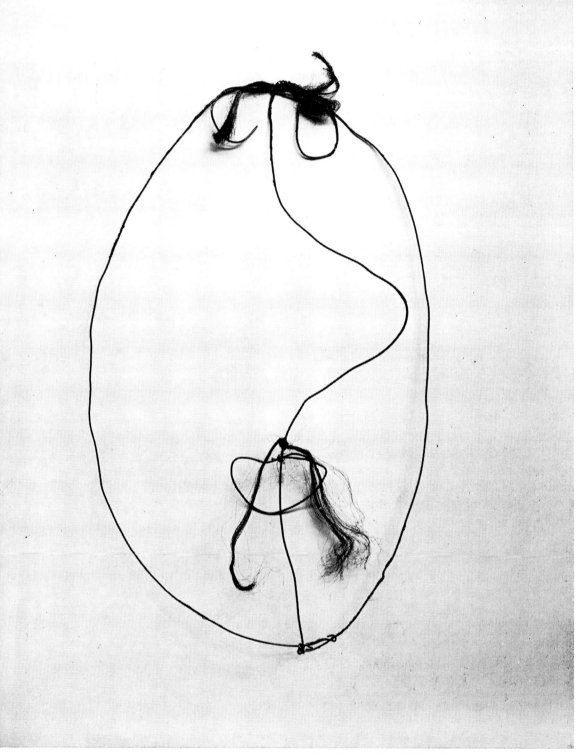

Wire Portrait (15" high) by Dan, grade 4; New Lincoln School, New York. In this humorous wire drawing, Dan created a third dimension by making the nose protrude from a flat oval face. He chose very fine wire for the hair and the moustache.

wire sculpture

drawing with wire—construction with wire

Adrienne, who is eight, said, "What a lovely wire painting. No, it's more like a drawing. It *is* a drawing." Adrienne was right, for drawing is what artists call the art of working with wire. Wire is a line, and a shape made with it is like a drawing except that the line is made of wire in the air instead of with pencil on paper. It is also called wire sculpture because it is usually three-dimensional. Some well-known contemporary artists use wire to create highly original works. Alexander Calder uses wire for portraits and animals and Richard Lippold uses it for abstract constructions.

Children work with wire in two ways: They make wire drawings which suggest subjects and they make abstract wire constructions.

Wire is an inviting material for children to use. "Can't I please have some wire to take home?" they often ask. "I just like to have it to make things from." They soon gain mastery over this medium, for it is flexible and easy to control, directly with the hands.

Because shapes made with wire are so easily altered, it is an excellent material to give a student who has had little experience with art materials. He can bend and rebend it until he is satisfied, thus building confidence in his own power to create new forms and to represent things that interest him.

Wire can be distributed in a crowded classroom and leaves no mess to be cleaned up. A simple request like, "Keep the wire on your desk and do not wave it around," has been a successful caution in many large classes.

Working with wire stimulates students who are experienced in art to be more inventive in the use of line. Paint, clay and pencil will inspire children to express personal reactions to people, animals or experiences, in terms of these media. In using wire for such subjects, children have the chance to develop new personal reactions that can be carried out only in wire. Because wire is a less familiar material than paint or pencil, some boys and girls may more easily show, through its use, individual impressions like the tallness of a person or the exaggeration of a gesture. Wire can also give a fresh and honest approach to drawing and combat the use of stereotypes and clichés.

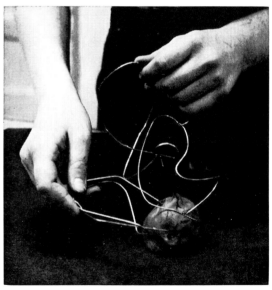

Photo: Hella Hammid

When older elementary and junior high school students, experienced with wire and other media, create with wire, the teacher can help them see that line is more than merely an outline; it can also go around, over and under a figure. Such observation can result in imaginative and individual use of line in all media.

73

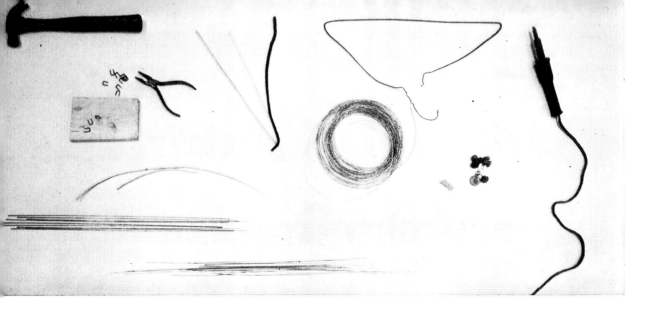

materials for wire sculpture

Wire is made from several metals and comes in various thicknesses called gauges. Contrary to what one might think, smaller numbers indicate thicker wires. Gauges between 10 and 16 can be used for most work, while a fine wire of 20 to 30 gauge is best for decoration and joining. For beginners, choose wire that is soft and easy to bend.

Iron wire from hardware stores is satisfactory and inexpensive; however, it is more convenient to use florist's wire, which comes in eighteen-inch lengths, obtainable from florist's supply houses. Florist's wire does not tangle or kink like coil wire and is easy to store and distribute to a class.

Copper wire is good but expensive, though scrap is sometimes given away by wire factories. Young children, particularly, enjoy working with colored pipe cleaners and bell wire which has a colored coating. Coated wire is also obtainable in various gauges from electrical supply houses. All of these wires, because they are soft, bend easily.

Older children can use coat hangers, either separately or combined with other wires. Baling wire and stovepipe wire are usable, too.

Junior high school students will enjoy using aluminum clothesline wire. It has the disadvantage of breaking easily but is interesting in combination with other wires and very good for large decorative work.

The basic tool for all work with wire is cutting pliers.

Young children may use a small piece of clay or plasticine for a base. Wire may be stapled to a piece of cardboard or attached with a paper fastener to form another kind of base. Older children can attach wire to a wood base, using staples (U-tacks) and hammer, or make a free standing form by bending the wires.

Young children may join wires by twisting two pieces together or overlapping two pieces and wrapping them with fine wire. Junior high school students enjoy learning to use an electric soldering iron. A piece of asbestos under the work will prevent the table being scorched. If available, a metal vise is useful for holding and flattening wire.

At times it will be stimulating to have available small items for decoration such as buttons, bits of screening, feathers, beads, bits of colored cellophane or gelatin and string.

wire sculpture in preschool and kindergarten

Young children are usually intrigued with wire and spontaneously explore it by twisting, bending and joining it together. The illustrations on this page show early stages of wire exploration. Four- and five-year-olds without previous experience will usually begin like three-year-olds but will move more rapidly toward working with more skill and planning.

Bright colored pipe cleaners and coated wires are an ideal introduction for preschool boys and girls. As children gain control, other soft pliable wires in a variety of lengths may be added. The materials are the motivation but the teacher may say, "How can you twist and join these wires to make shapes?"

Tanya, three years, twisted and bent some wires then found several ways she could join them together. She made many small pieces, working a long time on the white wire (above) to make it stand up.

Ned, four years, had more control and experience with materials. He started his construction (center) with a wire already stapled to a cardboard base. He carefully attached other wires to it and worked to make the shapes come out the way he wanted. The teacher commented on the arrangement of large and small shapes and the way his wire sculpture looked from all sides.

Elisabeth, five years, whose construction of pipe cleaners and wires is below, was concerned with problems of construction and arrangement as she skillfully joined the wires and pipe cleaners together to make her free-standing design.

A teacher encourages each child in his development by looking closely at the work, noting individual differences and by the descriptive comments she makes about ways children have made shapes and related them together.

First exploration of wire by Tanya, 3 years.

Photos: Lois Lord

Wire construction by Ned, 4 years, Bank Street School, New York.

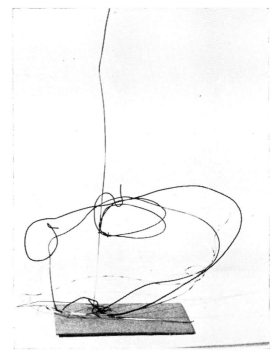

Wire construction by Elisabeth, 5 years, Bank Street School, New York.

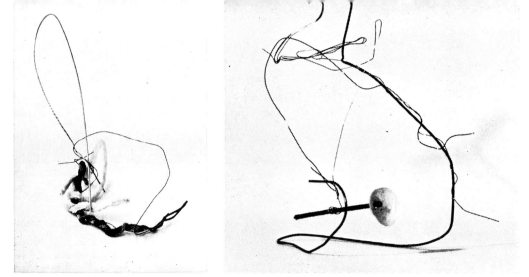

Left: Experiment by Ellen, grade 1 and Right: Wire Sculpture by Joe, grade 2,
New Lincoln School, New York. Ellen experimented by twisting pipe cleaners
and wires together so they would stand alone. Joe twisted a heavy
piece of wire so it made an interesting three-dimensional shape
and then joined fine wires to it. He made a contrasting accent
by adding a small shell attached to a stick.

wire sculpture in grades one and two

Most six-year-olds are able to use wire
easily. They are especially intrigued by long
colored pipe cleaners and bell wire with its
colored coating. They can also use soft,
uncoated wire.

Working with wire without other construction materials offers children the opportunity
to concentrate on problems of construction
and the relationship of shapes made with
line in space. If first and second graders have
not had previous experience they must be
given opportunity to explore wire as suggested
for younger children in the previous section.

The first experiments in twisting and bending wire have great value for children even
though they may produce nothing to display.
As they gain in experience their wire constructions will become more organized.

The teacher might introduce wire with such
suggestions as: "You can make designs with
wire. How can you bend it? What kind of
shapes can you make from it? How does it
look when you use both thick and thin wires?
You can make people and animals out of
wire too."

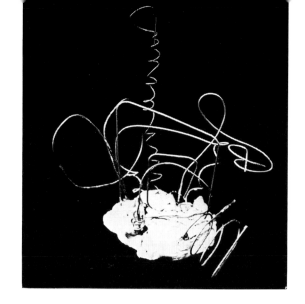

Thought Machine (7" high) by Jeff, grade 3; New Lincoln School, New York. Jeff found many ways he could bend and twist wire to make this three-dimensional design on a clay base; for example, he twisted the wire for the tall center spiral around a paintbrush handle. His construction is more complex and controlled than those illustrated at the top of the facing page.

A small piece of clay, plasticine or styrofoam makes a good base if a child wishes to have his wire stand up or he may start from a pipe cleaner or wire stapled to a piece of cardboard or wood. Some young children make flat wire drawings which later may be stapled or taped flat on paper or hung up with a string.

It is wise to let first- and second-graders realize that they have a choice between making representational or nonrepresentational shapes. The wire drawings of first- and second-graders do not have realistic proportions but are simple symbols, without detail, of people, animals, plants and objects. Some children will start with a specific idea in mind and tell what their figures are; others generalize, as Leslie did when she made *A Man*, middle of lower photo, Page 76. The child's ability to draw and paint figures will be the teacher's guide on how much to stimulate him to make wire figures.

Drawing with wire can sharpen observation and may inspire him in making personal and original symbols of what he knows and sees. These skills may often carry over to his work in other media. Constructing with wire gives a child the opportunity to explore more fully another three-dimensional medium and find out how he can organize and design with it.

← Left:
Wire People (7" to 3" high) by second-graders, Midtown Ethical Culture School, New York. These simple, flat figures show individual ways in which young children have used wire. *Left to right: Man Dancing,* by Tony; *Indian,* by Victor; *A Man,* by Leslie; *Hindu Lady,* by Rashmi; *Girl Jumping Rope,* by Pamela.

wire sculpture in grades three and four

By the time children are eight they have become more deeply involved in finding out what materials are really like and what they can do with them, for they have more skill and control than do younger children. At this point they are usually ready to use wire by itself. The wire constructions of experienced third and fourth graders are generally more clearly thought out, more complex in design and more carefully executed than those of younger children.

Wire is well suited to expressing both the real and the fantastic. Often the material itself suggests an idea. Jeff, who lacked confidence and often found it hard to get started, was merely twisting a piece of wire. Suddenly he said, "I am making a thought machine." This is illustrated above. He talked about it to his friend Bob and said, "The thoughts go in this coil, and then up to the radar." Bob said, "How do you make them do that?" Jeff replied, "I am making this so you can turn the handle." There was something intrinsic in this material that inspired Jeff to develop an idea as he worked and become involved in the technical problems necessary to implement his imaginative ideas.

Skier (12" high) by Agatha, grade 3; New Lincoln School, New York. Agatha started with two wires stapled to a wood base. She twisted the wires to make the legs and body and used thin wire to bind together wires added to form head, arms and ski poles. Like the wire drawings of most eight-year-olds, the figure is flat in concept though the arms and ski poles are set forward, giving it a limited third dimension.

It is good to have scrap wood for bases, with staples and a hammer available for attaching the wire. Wire can also be bent and attached with a paper stapler to a cardboard base. Some children like to start from wire already attached to a base while others prefer to make the wire shape and then tack it to a base. Still others prefer to work on a clay base.

As with first- and second-graders, the teacher first suggests experimentation. Then he makes the motivation broad enough to stimulate both those who prefer to construct abstract designs and those who prefer to make figures or fantasies. "What kind of shapes can you make with wire? How can you twist and bend it into a design?" or "Does it suggest something like a person, animal or machine to you?" are some questions the teacher might ask.

In making wire figures, eight- and nine-year-olds often start with an idea of a person in some particular action. They may develop this idea further as they work and add details. Agatha suggested hair, eyes and nose, with fine wire, on her skier, above.

After children have gained some experience, the teacher can help them bring out more ideas of their own with questions like these: "What kind of person will you draw with wire? Is he fat, short, or tall? Is he sitting, standing or is he doing something? What pets do you have: dogs, cats, birds? What other animals do you know? Think about one; what shape is it? Does it have short legs or long? What sort of tail or ears? How can you show these features with wire?"

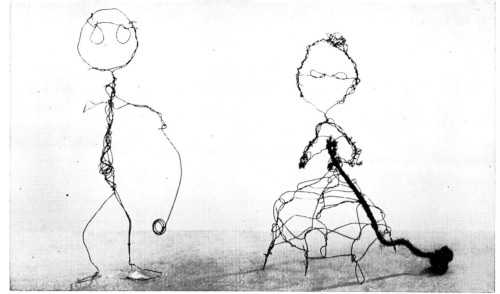

Wire Drawings (6″ high) by fourth-graders; Center School, New Canaan, Connecticut. Left, Boy with a YO-YO, by Nancy. This is a flat wire drawing which Nancy stood up by bending the feet. *Right, Woman Knitting, by Carol,* is more advanced in three-dimensional concept than the work of most fourth-graders. While the head is flat, the arms are brought forward and the skirt, made of several pieces of joined wire, is three-dimensional. In this way she solved the problem of making a sitting figure.

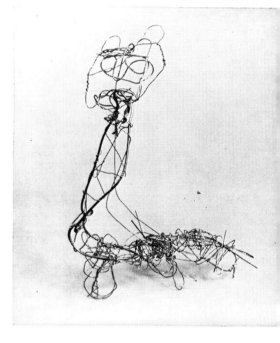

Animal (7″ high) by David, grade 3; Center School, New Canaan, Connecticut. David used thin and thick wire for this original animal in which the head and neck are flat but the body and legs have a three-dimensional quality because of the way the wires are twisted.

Man on a Tightrope (6″ high) by John, grade 4; Center School, New Canaan, Connecticut. John expressed with originality the tension of tight-rope walking. He loosely joined the wires forming the body of the man so that it moves at the waist when the rigid tightrope is manipulated.

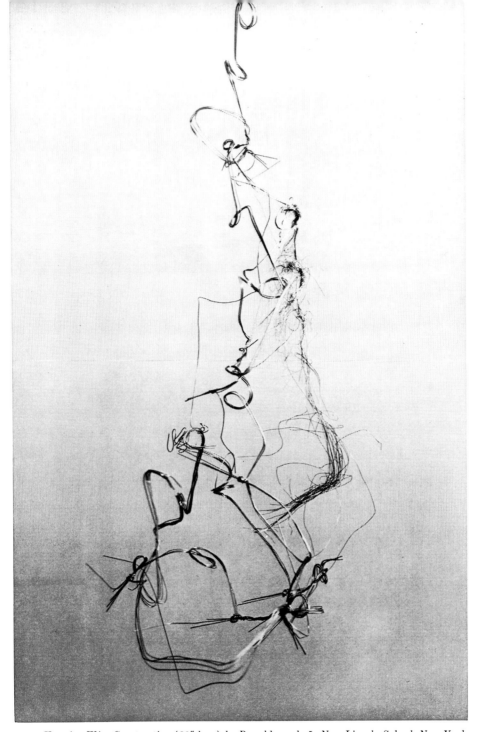

Hanging Wire Construction (20″ long) by Donald, grade 5; New Lincoln School, New York.
Donald's design is more complex and better organized than the work of many
children his age, and older. He repeated, with variation, the small twists
within the larger shapes thus creating rhythm and subtle relationships.

wire sculpture
in grades five and six

Fifth- and sixth-grade boys and girls find wire a particularly appealing and stimulating material. In addition, it offers progressive technical challenge yet is not too difficult for them to handle. It is adapted to the expression of humor and to the simplification of gesture or action. Because, by the age of ten or eleven, children have a longer span of attention, many of them will be capable of making more finished works than do younger children.

If fifth- and sixth-graders have not previously used wire, the same kind of approach should be taken as with younger children. Making wire constructions in the first session should give the children the chance to explore the material. At the same time the teacher might encourage them to think in terms of linear design, asking: "How can you make your wire line move in space? Can you make a design with large shapes and small shapes that seem to belong together?"

It is important that each child be guided to approach the material in the most personal way. It is more than likely that some individuals will experiment by making figures while others, like Donald, will make a construction, Page 80.

Some inexperienced children or those who in the past have been told exactly what do to, may need more specific help. For example, the teacher might say, "Here is one way you can join wires by twisting the ends together. Perhaps you can do this to add a piece to your construction or arms to your figure. Many of you will invent other ways of joining wires together." The teacher will be ready to help and encourage children while they work and will respond with pleasure to each different and individual interpretation of a subject.

To stimulate children who want to make wire drawings of people the teacher might say, "Think of some person and how you could make a wire drawing or caricature of him. Is the person tall? Then you could extend the wire,

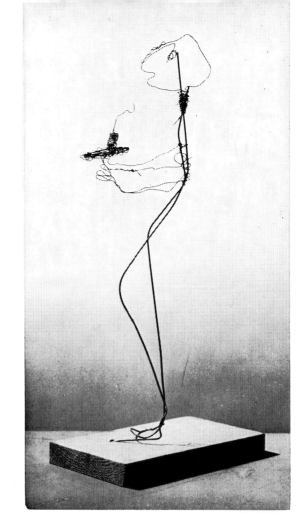

Waiter Carrying a Tray (12″ high) by Hilary, grade 5; Center School, New Canaan, Connecticut. Hilary achieved a three-dimensional quality by showing the head in profile, bending the legs and extending the arms which hold the tray far forward in the typical gesture of a waiter.

perhaps by joining two pieces to make him very tall. Or is it a short fat person?" Wire is an excellent material for depicting people in action as illustrated by *Woman Sweeping* and *Skater*, Page 83.

Some children will still use, at this age level, wood or cardboard bases for their wire; others, who are experienced, will be ready to make figures that stand alone. The teacher might challenge them with this question: "How can you make a piece of wire stand up by itself?" He may then suggest that wire figures can be made to stand alone.

The teacher may also point out that wire can be used to show the thickness of an object.

81

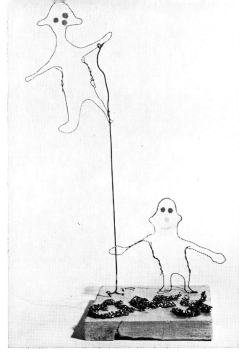

Circus Monkeys (18″ high) by Joy, 11 years; Museum of Modern Art Classes, New York. Joy enhanced her wire drawing by making the faces of transparent cellophane on which she pasted circles of red for eyes. She chose tinsel for the word "Circus" on the base.

During such a discussion one pupil said, "Oh, the great thing about wire is you can use it to make something two-D or three-D, whichever you want. You can even make an animal with a three-D body and a two-D head."

Boys and girls at this age take many ideas for their art from their own world. Therefore, classroom discussion about what goes on in the area, be it city, town or country, can stimulate ideas. As in all good discussions, one idea can lead to another so that each child will choose what interests him most for his wire drawing.

A teacher in New York City gave this as motivation: "What do you see and do in Central Park?" Each boy and girl made something different. Among the wire drawings were children skipping rope, running and batting a baseball, people sitting on a bench and dogs of many breeds.

Other suggestions might be: the zoo, the circus, people you see and what you do downtown, animals and people on the farm, the county fair or the airport.

Occasionally a class might enjoy a group project. This will involve planning the whole before work is started. The group might work out a setting with paper or other materials; then each child will contribute a figure, animal, plant, machine or building made of wire.

Giraffe (20″ high) by Chip, grade 6; New Lincoln School, New York. Chip was inventive in twisting, joining and shaping wire to make this imaginative, free-standing animal which he called *"Aloysius."*

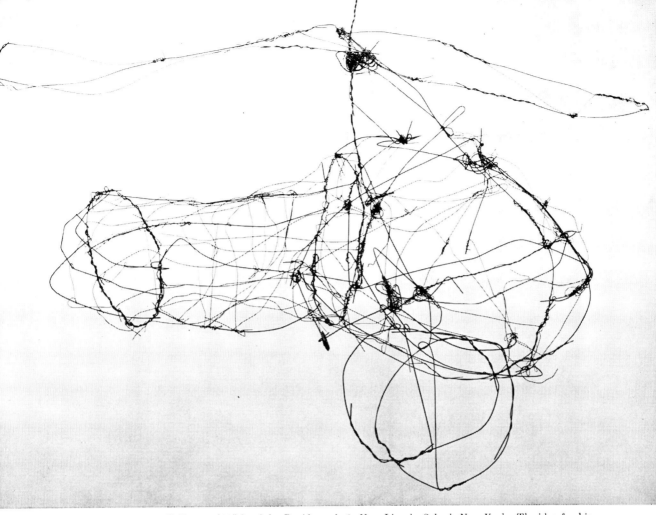

Helicopter (34″ long) by David, grade 6; New Lincoln School, New York. The idea for his construction came to David after a discussion about motion. He worked for several art periods joining 18″ lengths of thick and thin florist's wire to make this completely three-dimensional design.

People in action by fifth graders; New Lincoln School, New York. Below: Woman Sweeping by Barbara who simplified the figure in order to express the action of sweeping. *Left: Skater by Julie* who used thick wire to delineate action and fine wire to suggest the mass of hair and the clothing.

Photos: Lois Lord

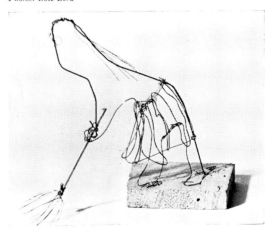

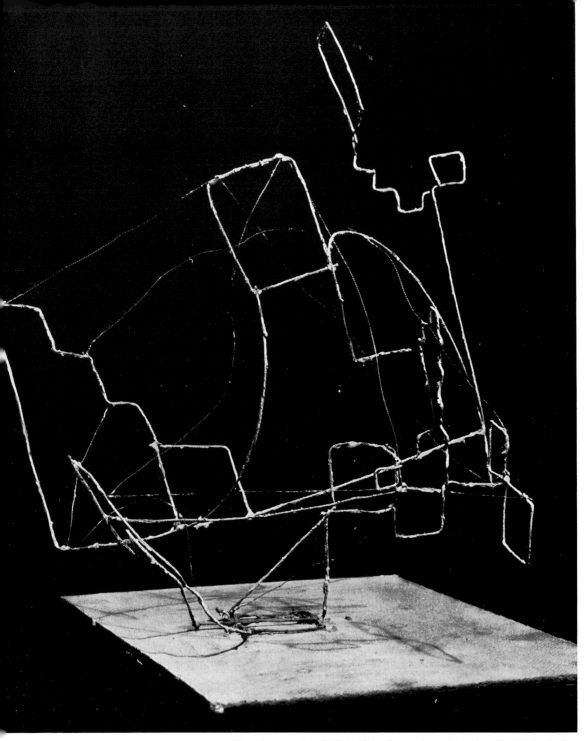

Wire Construction (18" high) by Leonard, grade 8; Rye High School, Rye, New York. Many junior high school students are able to make carefully thought-out, complex constructions. Leonard has soldered together thick and thin wires, forming angular shapes and curved lines related to each other in space. He coated some of the wires and the wood base with plaster which he painted magenta.

wire sculpture
in junior high school

The intrinsic quality of wire as an art medium offers a particular challenge to boys and girls in junior high school. Because it is less familiar than most media, they are more likely to approach it without the inhibiting standards many of them have for drawing with pen or pencil.

Wire offers to the inexperienced a new material which can be of absorbing interest because it can be used in a variety of ways, yet is not difficult to control. To the experienced, continuing drawing and constructing with wire can be the means to study line as an element of design and to develop further imaginative concepts of line as a way to express form and space.

In planning motivations, the teacher should keep in mind both the experienced and inexperienced. As in all media, a series of problems should be planned which increase the challenge to the students and at each step allow them to feel some accomplishment.

At this age most students need some specific suggestions because many of them no longer approach art with the spontaneity of young children. The first time wire is offered, a problem in construction using both thin and thick wire might be suggested by the teacher thus: "Experiment first with a small piece. Find out how you can curve and bend it. When you make your construction decide whether you want to use curved or angular shapes. How will you arrange them so they will belong together in one design? Keep turning your piece around, for you are making something three-dimensional that should look equally well from all sides."

At the next meeting of the class limits might be suggested such as making a construction with only curved or angular shapes; or each student may set limits for himself. Older students often react more imaginatively to a problem which definitely limits them.

Technical problems such as mastering all the ways that wire can be joined are challenging. Students will respect a standard for making joints as neat as possible. However, a teacher should never insist on careful technique until students are experienced enough to feel the need for it and realize that careful workmanship may make shapes appear more expressive. Using an electric soldering iron is especially intriguing to boys. It adds another tool to their mechanical experience and offers a stimulus to further invention and experimentation.

A ninth-grader using a soldering iron for his wire sculpture.

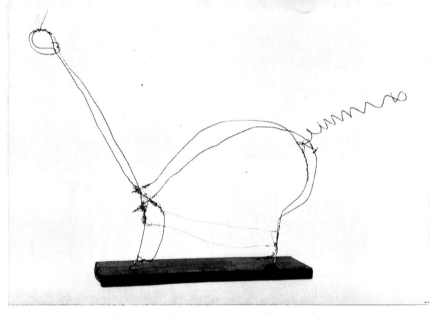

Imaginary Animal (16″ long) by John, grade 7; New Lincoln School, New York. A simple, expressive, three-dimensional shape in which the small head, long neck and twisted tail relate well to the shape of the body.

Although some seventh- and eighth-grade students will make flat figures, others will soon be ready to approach wire drawing in space. For example, Dan's *Indian* and John's *Animal*, illustrated on this page, although unsophisticated, would hardly be taken for the work of very young children because both were conceived, from the beginning, in the round. This ability to use line three-dimensionally should be kept in mind by the teacher who might motivate thus: "How can you show thickness of the body? Which lines will you choose? You can put the arms in any position, bent back or forward. Can you turn the head? How will you place the legs?"

Even though we expect most junior high school students to make their wire drawings three-dimensional, an experienced student may, at times, make a flat drawing with wire. This may be the right way for him to work, provided it is a real choice resulting from knowing other possibilities.

Some subjects that interest students of this age are dancing, games, characters from books or movies and portraits. In suggesting por-

Indian (9″ high) by Dan, grade 7; New Lincoln School, New York. Dan made this primitive figure three-dimensional by winding wires around the body and legs to achieve a feeling of bulk, and so constructed that it stands alone.

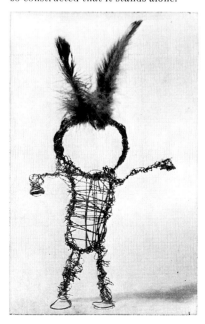

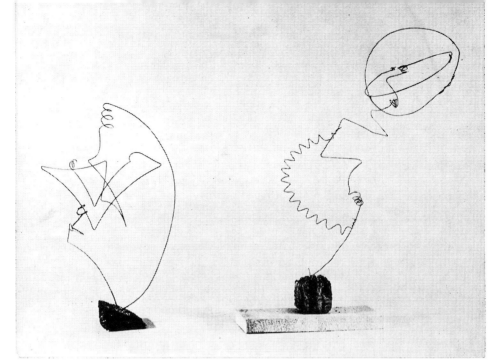

Portrait and Construction (6″ and 8″ high) by Steven, grade 8; Rye High School, Rye, New York.
By a continuous line moving in space, Steven indicated the shape and structure of
this caricature head. His construction, *right*, differs from Leonard's, Page 84,
in that he has emphasized linear quality, delicately poising the
construction on one slender wire based in a piece of cork.

*Couple Dancing (9″ high) by Sylvia, grade 8; Baron Byng
High School, Montreal, Canada.* The rhythm of dancing
is suggested by the relationship of lines which
describe the shapes of the two figures. Sylvia
put a gay blue cellophane skirt on the girl.

traits, the teacher could point out how line can
be used to indicate an expression or to show
the kind of person, thus: "Does the person you
want to portray have a young, round face or an
angular, old one?" or, "If you want to make a
caricature, then exaggerate some feature very
much." Steven, in his portrait above, made the
nose very large and the spectacles very small.
Chaffee, in his *Pianist*, Page 89, exaggerated
the gesture and the hair.

Ninth-grade students, whether experienced
or not, are usually able to go deep in the exploration of such material as wire. Of course
one material will appeal to some students more
than others. The teacher will continuously
point out qualities of linear design and expression which students achieve in order to
further their knowledge and stimulate growth.

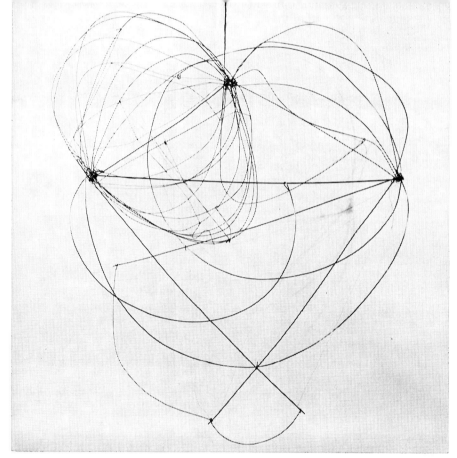

Hanging Wire Construction (19″ wide) by Douglas, grade 9; New Lincoln School, New York. Douglas created a harmony of circular and triangular forms by interweaving delicate and heavy wire.

Douglas, whose construction is illustrated, had never taken an art course and claimed he never liked art. Working with wire touched off a creative spark and he did a series of wire constructions, each more refined and personal than the last. He spent a great deal of time on these, even coming after school to work.

David had done a great deal in art but was too facile and his work tended to have a superficial quality. The teacher urged him to do more individual and thoughtful work, pointing out that he could use line in various ways to express action. After many attempts he produced the *Dancer*, top of facing page. This work gave him a deep sense of accomplishment.

The art teacher, by his enthusiasm and by discussing the qualities that make a wire sculpture a work of art, can arouse the students' curiosity so they will be interested in studying originals or reproductions of the work of Calder, Lippold and other artists who work in wire. Analysis of such works, after students have themselves explored wire, will help them understand these works and encourage them to search for further ways of developing their own wire sculpture.

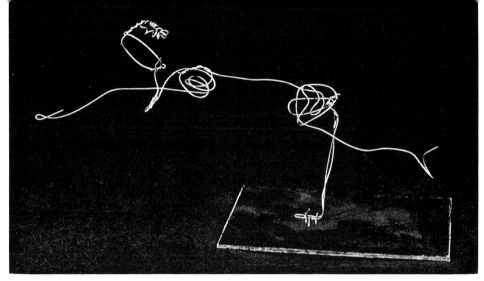

Ballet Dancer (7″ long) by David, grade 9; New Lincoln School, New York.
This figure is a completely three-dimensional expression. David attached
one leg to the cardboard base making the figure poised as if in motion.

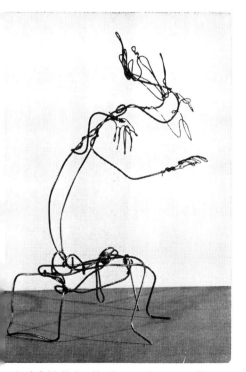

*Cockatoo (8″ high) by Rose, grade 9; Baron Byng
High School, Montreal, Canada.* A humorous wire
drawing in which Rose added colored wool to make
delicate, straight, decorative lines and a
bright feather for the tail.

*...nist (7″ high) by Chaffee, grade 9; New Lincoln
School, New York.* In this wire sculpture that
stands alone, Chaffee has dramatized
the action of a pianist.

Farm (14' long) by third-graders; Center School, New Canaan, Connecticut. Thirty children participated in making this collage mural in which a variety of textures and patterns were selected by the group. Before the group decided on the final arrangement, each child cut out shapes then pinned them to the colored paper background.

Winter in the City, Collage mural by first graders, P.S. 243, Brooklyn, N.Y. Each boy and girl made a person from collage materials. The teacher asked, "We cannot cover the thermostat so how can you make it part of your mural?" The children decided it would be the middle of the skating rink. Suggestions for imaginative symbolizations had included a manhole, the top of a garbage can. The texture of snow and ice was painted on the mural by a few children while others made collage buildings. The people were attached to the background when all children were satisfied with the arrangement.

Photo: Elaine Wickens

collage and construction in school activities

Art can become a vital part of the life of any school. Bulletin boards, murals, posters and special season and party decorations can be as expressive of the pupils as is their other art work. It is a wonderful challenge to the teacher to stimulate children to approach these projects with originality so the results will reflect the interests and ideas of those who have made them. When boys and girls are familiar with many materials, and have had developing creative experiences with collage and construction, they are able to approach many projects with greater originality than they would if their art experience had been limited to one medium, such as paint.

murals and bulletin boards

Collage is an excellent medium for group murals. It is effective because it can use large areas and simple shapes which are easily seen from a distance, and is in keeping with the flatness of a wall. Each child can contribute something he makes himself, according to his ability. After cutting out his shape a child can pin it temporarily to the background. The pieces can be

moved around until the group has decided on the final arrangement, the pasting being done by a few at the very end. The farm mural, above, was made by a group of thirty children. A mural can also give one child or a small group the opportunity to work with collage on a large scale as in the mural at the left which was made by two children. It is not always advisable for all the children in a group to participate in making a mural; four to ten at a time usually is a workable number.

The subject of a mural must be one which is of genuine interest to all the children participating. The subject chosen by a group may come from their life outside or inside the school. Art work related to the social studies is valid only when it results from real interest and enthusiasm on the part of the children. Sometimes children are so engrossed by what they are studying that they want to express their feelings about it. School subjects can often be as exciting as any others when children are expressing what they feel and not merely illustrating facts. Such projects are most successful when they originate with the students and when the classroom and art teachers work together from the beginning in giving them guidance.

The class which made the mural above chose a farm, something they knew well, because they live in the country. Other subjects which might be chosen by country children could include: playing in the woods, fishing, riding, harvesting the grain, activities in a dairy or the railway station.

City children have interests growing out of their particular environment. The teacher might ask them, "What part of the city do you find interesting?" Suggestions might include: downtown, the stores, a supermarket, factories, building a new apartment house, the subway, the playground. A mural could be based on one or several of such topics. If "downtown" were chosen, the teacher might stimulate more definite thinking by asking: "Each of you try to think of something you see or do downtown. What are the people doing? What kind of buildings are there? What do you see on the streets; in the park?"

Sometimes the size and shape of a mural are determined by the available wall space. In this case the design must be worked into the space at hand. At other times there is ample usable wall space and the mural can be planned in any dimension and shape that suits the subject and looks well on the wall. Backgrounds may be made from wrapping paper or from pieces of colored paper taped together.

The next step is for the group to choose materials they think would be most effective. It is important to have available both large and small pieces in a variety of textures and patterns. Pupils can also be encouraged to bring additional materials from home.

Once a subject has been selected and the size and shape decided upon, the teacher will encourage more specific thinking. If a city is the subject, the teacher could ask, "How might you arrange your city on this background?" One pupil might answer, "We could have big buildings," another adding "We must leave enough room for the streets because we want to put in lots of buses, cars and people." As the idea becomes clarified the children will be better able to decide what size to cut the objects. It is wise to encourage children to cut out the large shapes first. Small things and details can always be added later. Young children usually want the important things large. Older students often prefer more realistic proportions, though a teacher at times can point out that in design, exaggeration of size or shape may be used for emphasis.

Sometimes children apply three-dimensional materials as part of a mural or include mobiles or constructions, which are placed in front of the mural, as an integral part of the composition. In one school, fourth- and fifth-graders,

inspired by their study of animals, made a *Jungle* in which trees and plants were painted on paper; strange birds and bugs made from wire, gelatins, nets and other materials were suspended in front at different heights; and animals were free-standing on the floor, illustrated at bottom of facing page.

Arrangement of display or bulletin boards can be approached as a collage problem in terms of arranging shapes, colors, and textures in an interesting way. Collage may be combined with clippings to dramatize a news event; a display might consist of children's work; a collage, either abstract or representational, can be made to fill the entire space. In one high school, students each week design the bulletin boards in the corridors of the entire school. They have found that collage materials offer the greatest scope for originality, variety, effectiveness and interest.

A wall hanging which has many creative possibilities is one made from fabrics and yarns with the pieces stitched, rather than pasted, to a background. Some coarse material like burlap, either natural or colored, provides a good background. The wall hanging on Page 95 is composed of separate panels, each made by a member of a fifth-grade class. In de-

Leo the Lion, by Joe; detail from the jungle, right. Joe made a wooden saw-horse frame and formed his papier-mâché lion on it. He glued on cut-up yarn for the mane and tail.

Birds and a Bug; details from the jungle, below. Imaginary tropical birds and the bug were made from wire, bright colored tarlatan, colored tissue papers, metallic paper and feathers. The bird, *lower center*, was made from papier-mâché with collage materials.

Jungle, by a fourth- and fifth-grade group; New Lincoln School, New York. Each child made an animal to stand on the floor and one or more of the birds or bugs that hang from the ceiling. The animals, birds and free-standing trees suspended from the ceiling were made first because the children conceived the whole decoration in three-dimensional terms. Once these were in place, four children painted the background of trees and flowers in remarkably short time. All of the twenty-seven children in this group contributed ideas and work to the project.

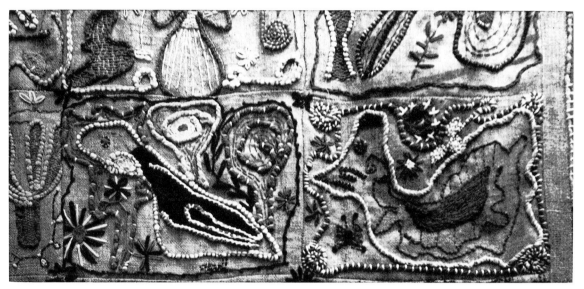

Detail from Wall Hanging, facing page.

scribing this project their teacher said, "Every child realized the problem in producing a fine design, then a new 'whole' evolved from arranging the many individual pieces." A stitched mural may also be made in the way suggested for a pasted one. Shapes of textured and patterned cloth, cut out by the pupils, may be arranged and pinned to the background and then a few children at a time may sew them on. At the end, details may be stitched in with yarn or thread.

The use of collage materials on a large scale, by groups and individuals, can be continued throughout elementary and junior high school. When a mural is being made the teacher must see to it that the group is not dominated by a few students and must help them realize that each pupil has something worthwhile to contribute. Occasionally, working in a group gives boys and girls an opportunity to discuss together choices of materials and placement of shapes, thus helping them become more aware of problems of composition.

Right: →

Cloth Wall Hanging by fifth-graders; Marlborough School, Kansas City, Missouri. Each child stitched a design from thick and thin yarns, creating his own textures and patterns. Finally the individual pieces were joined to form this unified design.

Photo: Art Department, Kansas City, Missouri, Public Schools.

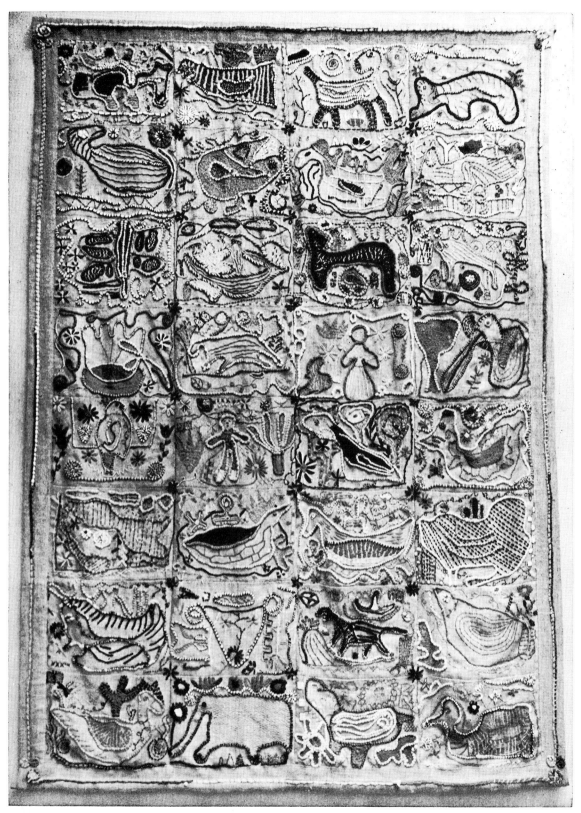

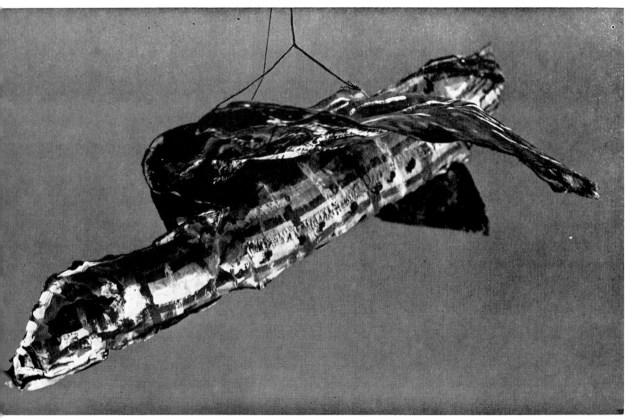

Bird (24" long) by a fifth-grader; West Seaford Elementary School, Delaware. "Follow the Birds to the Book Fair," read a simple sign by the front door. Many original birds made by children from grades four through six were suspended along the corridors. The shape for this bird was cut from a dry cleaner's paper dress bag, then stuffed with newspapers to make it three-dimensional. Wings were added and the bright pattern painted on last of all.

posters and greeting cards

Special events in school may be announced with posters or with three-dimensional constructions. The bird, above, shows one of many different birds made by fifth-graders to lead the way to the school book fair. Murals can be made to announce school events. Parties can be advertised by mobiles hung throughout the school. In one school a basketball game was publicized by three-dimensional figures made of wire mesh tacked to a bulletin board; the essential lettering, cut from colored paper, was stapled behind the transparent figures. To call attention to an art exhibit, a large construction, designed with various materials, stood on the floor in the lobby;

arrows, made from collage material, led through the corridors to the exhibit. These ideas are only a few of many ways in which three-dimensional materials may be used to publicize school events. Through making interesting materials available and by stimulating discussion a teacher can help students approach such tasks in fresh and original ways.

Since posters demand a bold style with simple, definite shapes which may not be in accord with a child's own style in painting, it is better to give him the medium of collage to which such a style is inherent. Class discussion can bring out the purpose of a poster and the kind of design that is suitable.

Poster (9″ x 12″) by Susie, grade 9; New Lincoln School, New York. In this well designed poster, Susie was able to give a feeling of dancing and gaiety by the way she placed shapes of red and pink cellophane in relation to white yarns, used to symbolize winter and dancing.

A poster must be striking so that the message will be visual and comprehended at a glance. A teacher can guide pupils in understanding that a striking design is simple, with few colors and materials, and strong contrasts. "How can you get strong contrasts?" the teacher might ask. Answers should include the following: dark and light, dull and bright color, large and small shapes, and rough and smooth material. Contrast and simple, clear organization of the design make it possible to see a poster from a distance or when one is moving rapidly. Lettering should be an integral part of the design. The verbal message should be given in as few words as possible. It has been found useful to suggest that boys and girls first work out the lettering on strips of tracing paper the size and shape to fit the design. After placement of the lettering has been decided, the words can be traced and painted or, better still, the letters can be cut from colored paper and pasted to the design. Collage offers the advantage of working out a design directly with the materials themselves. To make a preliminary pencil sketch for a poster is seldom satisfactory because it often results in small drawings with too much detail. The teacher may encourage pupils to symbolize the subject of a poster rather than make a literal or descriptive picture of it.

Mother's Day Card (7½" x 10") by Stefi, grade one; New Lincoln School, New York. Stefi effectively arranged patterned and colored papers and cellophane which she chose for her design. She applied one piece three-dimensionally.

Many children who normally work in original ways tend to rely on stereotypes when they make greeting cards. Such children may need special stimulation to approach designing greeting cards which are different in idea and execution from banal commercial cards. Stefi, whose card is shown above, spontaneously made it on a day when the class was working on collage. The principle of design for a card is the same as that of a poster except that, because a card is held in the hand, it may be more delicate and detailed, if the child wants it that way. Some special materials like gold and silver paper, delicate tissues, small colored stickers, and bits of lace may be saved in a special box for greeting cards. When encouraged to work in their own way, some children will choose to do abstract designs for their cards while others prefer to represent a subject.

Collage can also suggest some original approaches to making valentines. Some children, when they feel it will be acceptable, may choose to do abstract collage valentines. Those who want to use a heart motif should be encouraged to think of it as an element in a design which can be used in a variety of sizes, textures and patterns and arranged in many exciting ways.

A second-grader, who lately had experience with constructions, suggested to the teacher that, instead of cards, the group make "three-D" valentines. Valentine mobiles might be used as gifts or made large for decorations.

Valentine (12" high) by Joan, grade two; New Lincoln School, New York. To make this well composed construction Joan shaped wires and joined to them sticks and hearts cut from bright colored cardboard and nets.

Wire Sculpture Favors by students at Westport High School, Kansas City, Missouri. These lively wire figures portray various school activities.

Photo: Kansas City, Missouri, Public Schools

decorations for special holidays and parties

Materials can inspire boys and girls to find their own ways of expressing a holiday or a season. Too often the making of holiday decorations is forced upon children, resulting in the repetition of outworn forms like stereotyped tulips in the spring or turkeys for Thanksgiving. This is not an art experience; it will benefit children to make decorations for a special season only when they express some aspect of it that is vital to themselves.

Through discussion of the origin and atmosphere of a holiday, a teacher can evoke ideas from pupils which may be expressed in collage or construction.

Parties are often an important part of the extracurricular life of a school, especially at the junior high school level. Making decorations for parties can be an important extension of the art program. Decorating a room is essentially a problem in space design and should be approached as such. A simple cardboard model of the room to be decorated will often help students focus on the problem of how the space can be used and how it can be modified or changed to give the desired atmosphere. A few three-dimensional designs suspended in a room often do more to create an atmosphere than many flat decorations on the walls.

By using their knowledge of three-dimensional materials in making decorations for holidays and parties, students can make exciting designs and broaden their art experience by applying it to practical problems.

autumn

To many children Halloween suggests the fun they have that night rather than the traditional witches and pumpkins. A discussion may bring out ideas such as, children on the street, at a house for "trick or treat," or a Halloween party. If, on the other hand, the pupils seem more intrigued by the origin of Halloween, the discussion could bring out such subjects as, a mysterious night, a scary forest, or a lonely road. Any of these might be expressed in individual pictures, in group murals, constructions, or bulletin board decorations made with collage materials.

Masks are worn almost everywhere on Halloween, and even first-graders can make simple ones from colored paper or cardboard on which collage materials can be applied. A party held at school could be started by making masks. Paper bags, large enough to go over the head and decorated with collage materials, make a simple mask. Larger masks similar to David's, illustrated below, make effective decorations hung on the wall or suspended from the ceiling. Wall masks can also be constructed with large pieces of colored paper joined to form cylinders like the one illustrated, right. Sometimes, by using new materials, traditional symbols can be expressed in a fresh way. For example, the wire witch on Page 101 was one of many used to decorate a school cafeteria.

Many of the ideas mentioned above could be themes for a school dance. At one junior high school, students used *Scary Forest* as a dance theme. They made tree trunks of various diameters from two long pieces of wrapping paper, stapled together down the sides. Before stapling the second side, a long piece of wood and crushed newspapers were put inside so the trees stood up, firmly wedged between floor and ceiling. From the trunks long branches of paper were extended across the room and strange birds and bats, made from wire mesh and other materials, dangled from the ceiling.

Mask by David, grade 6; New Lincoln School, New York.
David made this mask to disguise himself on Halloween. He constructed a cylinder by stapling together the ends of a piece of corrugated cardboard, then attached the three-dimensional nose, mouth and decorations of yarns, feathers and cloth.

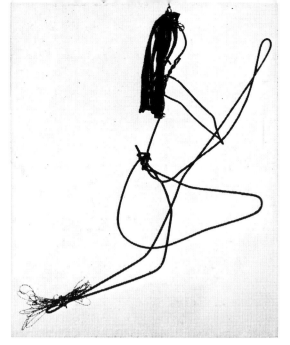

Witch (15″ long) by a ninth-grader; Tower Hill School, Wilmington, Delaware. This original witch, one of many used to decorate the school cafeteria, was made from coat-hangers. Cloth was cut and added for hair and fine wire made the end of the broom.

Wall Mask (36″ long) by fifth-graders; Center School, New Canaan, Connecticut. This mask is one of a series made for Halloween decorations. The cylindrical shapes are colored paper to which the children attached additional forms made of paper and collage materials.

Another junior high school group combined the themes of fall and Halloween to decorate the gym for a dance. Leaves cut from textured and transparent materials were hung on invisible strings across the room. Nylon fish line is excellent for this purpose. Goal posts were temporarily erected at either end of the room. Skeleton-like football players which wore only boots and helmets of colored paper were placed on top of the goal posts and around the walls of the room. The whole arrangement gave a weird and fanciful effect.

In discussing Thanksgiving, boys and girls usually have ideas connected with autumn, harvest, food or family dinners. Patterned, textured and transparent materials in a variety of colors can inspire them to carry out such ideas in original ways. A series of collage murals in which imaginary fruits and vegetables were made from such collage materials decorated the bulletin boards at Thanksgiving in one school. Visual interest was achieved by the contrast of size and placement of shapes as well as the choice of color and the use of pattern and transparency.

Christmas Tree (6' high) by Bob and Jim, grade 9; New Lincoln School, New York.
The designing of this Christmas tree came as a direct result of time spent
by the class making a variety of constructions. These two boys worked out their
idea together. They made pyramidal sections of balsa wood, then added
various colored yarns to make the free linear pattern. Finally
the parts were suspended one within another so they rotate.

winter

Christmas suggests bright and glistening materials for decorating school lobbies, classrooms and auditoriums. Christmas tree ornaments of wire, colored gelatins, metal papers and other collage and construction materials may be made by children of all ages, either for use at school or to take home. Most children enjoy taking a mobile home for the holidays.

In some cities fire regulations forbid the use of live Christmas trees. Children who have had experience with making constructions have shown ingenuity in constructing forms suggestive of trees. A few examples are given here. The mobile illustrated at the right could have many variations such as limbs made of wire or thin dowels, and decorated with thin wire or shapes made of gelatin, paper, wire mesh or other construction materials.

A Christmas tree of string can be made this way: Stick an adhesive picture hook to the ceiling and tie to it about twenty lengths of colored string. Tape the lower ends of string to the floor in a large circle, thus forming a cone shape suggestive of a Christmas tree. If this idea is suggested to students they should decide how to carry it out. Fine string will be invisible and the ornaments, which may be solid, shiny or transparent, will make the design in space and produce the effect of a tree. If heavy string or colored tape is used, the effect will be different. A variety of designs could be worked out with colors, lighting and ornaments.

A simple tree can be made quickly from wood by nailing slats of varying lengths to an upright. The slats should be painted or covered with thin, colored or metallic paper cut into shapes to suggest branches. Decorations made by pupils can be put on last.

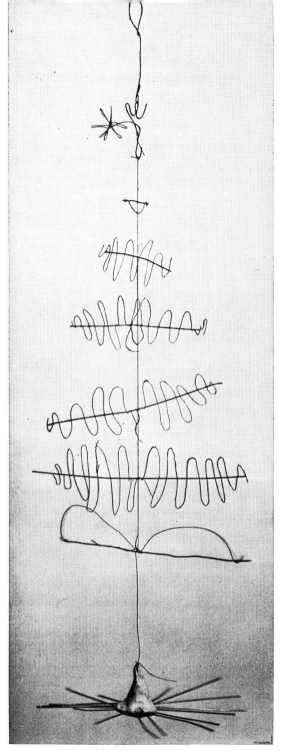

Christmas Tree (9′ high) by junior high school students; New Lincoln School, New York. In this mobile, lengths of aluminum clothesline wire, decorated with fine wire, suggest branches. They were suspended by string so they would swing in different directions.

Angel (23″ high) by a sixth-grader; West Seaford Elementary School, Delaware. This original angel, one of several suspended from the ceiling, was formed of basket reed to which was glued white tissue paper and the tinsel decoration. The eyes and mouth dangle on threads.

Photo. Ellsworth J. Gentry.

Christmas Mobile (30″ long) by a sixth-grader; West Seaford Elementary School, Delaware. Basket reed decorated with tinsel made the main shape. The stars, made by joining popsicle sticks, were brightly painted and suspended on threads so they would move.

Crèche (18″ high) by seventh-graders; Tower Hill School, Wilmington, Delaware. These figures were constructed with wire and copper, brass and aluminum foil.

A group of first-graders made huge trees to decorate the walls of their auditorium, one of which is illustrated, right. A few children sketched the outlines with chalk on wrapping paper, then painted them. On some trees they applied the paint in texture with sponges. Each child made ornaments of shiny and textured transparent materials and stapled or glued them to the trees.

Mobiles are appropriate to the gaiety of the Christmas spirit and, if planned around a theme or color scheme, can be the main decoration in the school or for a party.

Themes from the story of Christmas can be expressed in many ways with three-dimensional materials. The crèche illustrated at the bottom of Page 104 is one example. Chanukah, the lighting of the candles, or the lion and the menorah can be expressed in a number of ways with a variety of materials.

It is important to discuss all the ideas that this season suggests to the children. The religious origins, winter, and the season of the year will recall to many the things they do: singing, shopping, winter sports or parties. Any of these could be developed in original ways with two- or three-dimensional materials.

Some themes that have been used for Christmas parties are *Winter Wonderland*, in which trees were cut from white corrugated cardboard and blue and transparent cellophane icicles hung from the ceiling; *Winter City* was expressed by abstract buildings of collage materials placed on three-fold screens. Windows were suggested with red and yellow metallic paper. From the ceiling hung simple mobiles of metallic papers to suggest city lights and in the center of the room there was a huge mobile Christmas tree. Fantastic toys made from construction materials, suspended from the ceiling and placed about the walls, carried out another theme. Abstract white paper sculptures effectively decorated the room for still another Christmas party.

Christmas Tree (7' high) by first-graders; Center School, New Canaan, Connecticut. To the paper shape, cut out and painted by a few children, each child glued ornaments made from collage materials.

spring

To children in the country, spring may suggest plants, birds, picnics or exploring in the woods; to city children, street games, the park or an excursion to the country may be significant of this season. Different colors and materials may appeal to different children: transparencies, bright tissue papers, subtle patterns, or delicate construction materials.

Delightful hats can be made from colored paper embellished with collage materials. Children who have made three-dimensional forms from paper will be able to extend such experiments into making unusual shapes for hats.

Making hats can be enjoyed by boys and girls in both elementary and junior high school. At one junior high school it was planned that everyone come to a dance wearing a hat. The boys worked for days beforehand making weird hats from wire and other construction materials while the girls made more feminine versions of paper, decorated with collage materials. Hats can be made at Easter or any other time of year, before a party or as an activity during the party program.

A room was decorated for a spring dance with imaginary plants and birds. The birds of different sizes were suspended at various heights, some very high, some very low, thus creating in the space a feeling of movement. The birds were made of wire, gelatins and thin colored papers so the shadows cast upon the walls were colored.

The theme for a party does not always have to relate to a holiday or season. Students accustomed to approaching many media with invention will learn to come up with ideas which they can carry out three-dimensionally. Some themes that have been worked out with construction materials are: a jungle, a carnival, under the sea, starry night, rocket to the moon. A dramatic theme for a dance in a school auditorium was one in which huge mobiles in a variety of sizes were suspended from the high ceiling. These were composed of abstract shapes built from slats of wood, covered or partly covered with gelatins in different tones of red. A few spotlights were directed on the mobiles so that red shadows cast on the walls made the whole room appear to be a mysterious place, full of movement and gaiety.

Where fire laws limit the use of paper decorations, teachers should see to it that students spray all paper and cardboard with a flameproof solution. If students are properly encouraged they will discover many ways in which to design with materials, thus changing a drab room into one that has the desired atmosphere for a party.

106

Children in a New York City Public School are inventive in making hats from a variety of papers.
Photo: Board of Education, City of New York.

Mask by Elliot, grade 6, New Lincoln School, New York. Elliot used wire mesh, strips of metal, wire and sticks to make this fantastic mask.

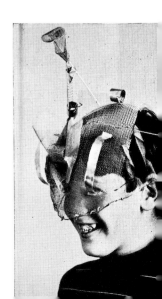

Fifth-graders at New Lincoln School, New York are using a variety of materials to express their own ideas.

to the teacher

The teacher is important because he makes possible an atmosphere wherein boys and girls can develop their creativeness and imagination.

A teacher who enjoys and understands children will learn to respect and understand their art work, if it is truly their own, even when it appears immature. A teacher's first step in understanding is to realize that it is an art experience for a child when he organizes materials in his own way to express something from his own experience or imagination. Each child should be encouraged to make all decisions himself for his art. Each time he does so he will gain increasing confidence to make further decisions.

A child's work is not his own when he copies others or when he uses stereotypes or clichés. In art, these are shapes or symbols hackneyed by previous use, as for example, cartoon people or animals, lifeless rabbits for Easter or conventionally stylized trees.

In helping children a teacher is guided by his knowledge of how they work with materials at different ages and by the fact that there are developmental differences among children of the same age. As is indicated throughout this book, children must start where they are.

A child will be deprived of the opportunity to grow if adult ideas are imposed on him or if he is expected to work in a way that is beyond him. For example, if a young child, who is at the stage of drawing people by symbols, were asked to draw a figure in "correct" proportions his natural development would be retarded. If this has happened to a child, a teacher can help him recover. A third-grade teacher, whose class felt inadequate in art and therefore did not like it because they had previously been given work beyond them, had this experience: One child explained, "We can't make houses and trees like the other teacher told us." This teacher introduced collage, which was new to them. She found they were able to approach it without fear and enjoyed the materials. After several experiences they learned to compose the materials in individual ways. Later they were able to use other materials with more freedom and finally, to paint from their own experiences at their own level.

If only accurate representation of factual material is expected from a child, he is being prevented from using his own curiosity and vision. It is the responsibility of the teacher to encourage him to use materials to express the way he sees, imagines or feels about something that deeply interests him.

Composition, the sensitive arrangement of shapes and colors, is fundamental to all art. Very young children have an intuitive feeling for such organization. If they are encouraged always to strive independently to arrange materials in good relationship, they will be likely to develop aesthetic sensitivity. A child can be "busy" pasting or hanging materials without being personally involved in the activity. If he is only busy it is not an art experience and the activity and resulting collage or mobile will be without life or meaning.

Collages and constructions, representational or abstract, can be as expressive of a child's personality and vision as his painting or clay

work, if he has been truly involved in working in his own way.

At times a child's art experience may not result in a product for display. He may have been exploring materials or perhaps "spoiled" his piece by experimental overworking. He deserves the same respect for such honest effort as he would receive for a beautiful result. Teachers should not feel pressure to display children's work, but rather be guided by what most benefits each child.

Children need the support of teachers and parents for creative growth. They are sensitive to approval or disapproval, whether voiced or not, and will generally strive for that which is approved. Teachers who understand this, value many kinds of art expression because they recognize that they are the children's best efforts, in their own style, whether skilled or first experiments. A teacher equally esteems, from different children, work that is bold or detailed and work that is representational or abstract.

Some parents, eager to learn about and appreciate their children's work, find it difficult to accept art forms unfamiliar to them. Therefore, it is important for teachers to interpret to parents the values for children, as explained earlier, of experimenting with materials and making collages and constructions.

Children need encouragement to develop and work to capacity. Therefore, teachers should develop a plan and organization for their art program. Some children find it frustrating to be given materials without any stimulation or suggestion. These children need to be inspired so they will find ways to use the material; others need help in bringing out their own ideas to avoid copying their own work or that of others.

A flexible art program should include both two- and three-dimensional experiences and all the materials that are suited to each age group. While there must be an over-all plan for the art program originating with the teacher, a pre-planned program covering a school year is not suitable because it cannot take into account all of the growing interests of a particular group. A teacher should be ready to modify any plan and follow the development and interests of the children. In one fourth-grade group the teacher had planned to follow collage with painting but the children started to use some of the collage materials three-dimensionally. This indicated that they were ready for a three-dimensional experience, so at the next lesson the teacher provided materials for constructions. After several sessions with constructions they went to clay. In clay work the children became interested in modeling people and animals. Then, many of them wanted to make paintings of some subjects in which they had become interested; this was, therefore, a desirable time to introduce painting.

There are advantages in presenting, at times, one medium to a whole group. Even though each child works in his own way, they gain inspiration from each other when there is a real atmosphere of discovery and invention. When a whole group works with one material, often a timid child finds courage to try something new which he would not have done on his own.

The aim in offering children many different materials is to give boys and girls a broad experience and to help each child find the medium best suited to him and his ideas. Some ideas

Porcupine by Benjamin, grade 3;
New Lincoln School, New York.

are best expressed in paint, some in clay, some in construction or collage materials or wire. A child cannot make intelligent choices if he has merely sampled many media and has not had time to discover the possibilities in each. Therefore, it is advisable to devote several consecutive lessons to each material so the teacher can help children have a deep experience with each medium. Thus, a deepening knowledge of materials can be acquired throughout the growing years.

In planning an art program the teacher, by presenting materials in a logical sequence, can help children understand that there is a fundamental relationship among all art media. For example, it would be logical to do wire sculpture

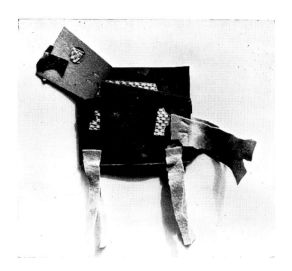

either before or after drawing with pen or pencil. Painting relates closely to collage and, as a natural result of making collages, children often paint with greater richness of pattern or texture. Children can be helped to realize that there are common problems in working with clay and constructions but the kind of design is determined by the limitations and possibilities of each material.

At times, the teaching plan for children above fourth grade may be based on their need to develop observation and ability to draw. For example, in one sixth grade the children were hesitant to draw people and asked for help. The teacher started with a suggestion of making people of collage materials, and in this medium they worked with more freedom. While discussing the position of figures playing games, the children took some poses characteristic of games in order to study the action. They then expressed the poses in clay and later made figures with wire. Finally, they felt experienced enough to make paintings of subjects with figures in action.

The aim in motivation is to strike a chord in each child that will evoke an idea which is important to him. If children's work merely illustrates what the teacher has said or done, each child's creative depth has not been tapped. For example, if a teacher merely gives "a farm" as a subject, every child may make a farmhouse. Whereas, if the farm had been the subject of class discussion by teacher and pupils, each child would have recalled something of personal interest and the resulting paintings might have included the following: animals, the cow barn, the farmer at his tasks, chickens being fed, inside the farmhouse. The discussion might also have suggested to some children subjects unrelated to the farm: the nearby town on Saturday night, a game or a dance.

A teacher will be delighted when a child comes to class with his own idea and does not need to find one through suggestions from him.

Sometimes motivation can be given which allows a choice of media to express ideas brought out through discussion. Usually it is not desirable to have more than three media available to the pupils at one time. The exact number will be determined by the teacher who will be guided in his decision by the number of pupils needing help at the same time and by the physical arrangement of the room. It is also of primary importance to both teacher and pupils that materials be kept in good order and easily available to the children.

In addition to planning a program and starting a discussion at the beginning of a lesson, a teacher can help boys and girls while they work. Sometimes a child needs further individual help, after the discussion, in order to

Collage Puppet by Jocelyn, grade 1, P.S. 166 Manhattan, New York.

get started. Perhaps he lacks courage to start something new, the discussion may have missed his particular interest, or he may have an idea and not know how to express it. Often the teacher, by asking a question or in some cases making a direct suggestion, can help such a child get started.

A teacher will be ready to give a nod of encouragement or a word of advice whenever it is needed. Children do not like to be hovered over while they work; they work best with the knowledge that help from the teacher is at hand when needed and that they have his support and confidence. As long as children are personally involved in what they are doing, they should feel free to experiment and try out materials in their own way and at their own speed. When a child asks for help it should be given in such a way that he makes the final decision for himself. For example, when a child asks the teacher what material he should put in an empty area of a collage, the teacher could discuss with him the possibility of repeating a

material already used or introducing something new. Thus, the child is helped to try out several possible solutions and make the final choice for himself.

If a child does not appear to be involved in his work, his interest can often be rekindled by the teacher who may talk to him about his idea and ways in which he would like to express it. A teacher can also help the child who is too easily satisfied with a poor effort by pointing out positive quality in his work and then suggesting possible ways in which he can continue with it.

In helping boys and girls with their art, the teacher tries to awaken the inner creative self of each one. He will be guided in what to say and do by his knowledge of the age, experience and capability of each pupil. Young children generally work intuitively and should be spoken to in simple terms. As they grow older, children often like more detailed analyses of their intuitive judgments and will want to know the reason why some arrangements seem more expressive or of better design than others.

The final important point in teaching art is the way the teacher feels about the finished work and the comment he makes about it. Children sense the feeling of adults and rightly suspect indiscriminate praise. While a sensitive teacher accepts the best effort of each boy and girl, his commendation will be based on the way a child has achieved some particular quality in his work or on the way he has used or experimented with the materials. For example, the teacher may praise the originality of an idea and the way colors and shapes have been used to express it, or he may commend the choice of materials and the way in which they have been designed and put together. Self-confidence is essential to growth. If a teacher can help a child to value the qualities of expression or design he has achieved, it will very likely motivate that child to put his effort into further creative development.

By giving children guidance and providing them with continuity of two- and three-dimensional art experiences, teachers can help children to have richer lives throughout the school years.

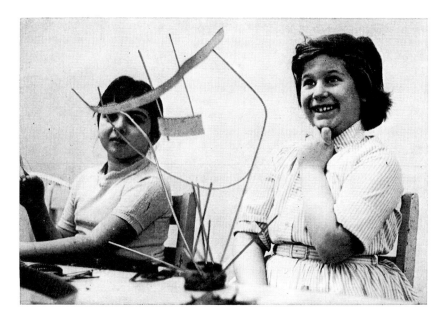

Photo:
Hella Hammid